Raising My Voice: The Memoir of an Immigrant, expanded my perspective in so many ways. Simona's vulnerable stories and authentic shares showed me a side of the world I have never truly experienced. I could feel myself in the scenes of her life and it caused me to look more seriously at my own. This gripping book had me take a look at how I can help eliminate discrimination and become a better ally to all of my brothers and sisters across the globe. If you are looking to be educated and inspired, look no further.

—Abigail Gazda
CEO of Hearts Unleashed

If someone has any doubt about the power of perseverance and positive thinking they need to read *Raising My Voice: The Memoir of an Immigrant* by Simona Spark.

Simona tells her compelling story, one of survival but also one of thriving, as she takes you through her experiences as a single mother who is fleeing her abusers and immigrating to the United States. Being a single parent it's daunting enough, but coupled with trying to build a life for her and her son, while learning to speak English will try the strongest of us. The added twist to try and hinder her success was the consistent and constant reminder, she was given by her abusers that she was not worthy and would not succeed.

Simona explains that these experiences are what has led her to what she is today. A very successful relationship coach living her best life and encouraging others to rise above and become the best as well. The value she brings to her clients isn't just from training she has received, but from experiences she has lived. I strongly encourage others to read this book. It is a testament of survival that will encourage and empower you to live an authentic life even if it means leaving your comfort zone to do it.

—Betsy Cairo, PhD, HCLD, CSES
Executive Director at Look Both Ways, Inc.

This book is an engaging tale of overcoming adversity and living an authentically fulfilled life. The stories are rich in content and the lessons are rich in inspiration. And to think that a few short years ago, Simona didn't even speak English. Remarkable!

—Bill Baren
Business Oracle at billbaren.com

In *Raising My Voice* Simona's story is evidence that when you follow the heart's call to freedom, you can overcome any obstacle and create the life of your dreams. Reading her story will have you feel that no matter what challenge you are facing in your life right now, you can succeed. Simona will teach you how the powerful inner work of facing, healing, and releasing trauma can help you become the person you are meant to be, and she will show you how to choose yourself in any circumstance. With Simona's story as your guide, you will begin to believe that you can triumph and fulfill your life purpose.

—**Carey Peters**
Co-founder of Health Coach Institute

Raising My Voice is a vibrant representation of the daily struggles many immigrants in search of better opportunities face while trying to adapt to a foreign country. From communist Romania to free enterprise America, she adequately portrays the qualities required to survive and succeed in a new country: hard work, tenacity and resiliency among others. Her story will definitely resonate with many of us who have experienced the challenges of moving our lives from one country to another either by choice or by necessity.

In addition, although it is an agonizing process, Simona does an amazing job at describing her personal emotional journey. She powerfully recounts the pain she and her son suffered at the hand of their domestic abuser, the power necessary to leave the relationship, and finally the determination it took for her to reclaim freedom and happiness. It is refreshing to see someone overcome so many hardships and still manage to show enough vulnerability to share her personal story with the rest of the world.

As an immigrant advocate and a mother, myself, I have a deep admiration for Simona's display of strength and perseverance which led her, without a doubt, to the successful career she is now embracing. Even if it was not at the best time in life for her, I'm sincerely grateful we met and that I was able to use my skills when she needed them most. I will always use her as an example in trying to help others in need.

—**Catherine A. Bauer**
Attorney at Law BAUER LAW FIRM, LLC

Raising My Voice is a gripping, courageous, downright heart wrenching novel about overcoming adversity, and discovering the untapped powers we have within ourselves. It is filled with wisdom, inspiration, and a profound message of self-empowerment. It's a book that will call you forth to deeper levels of empathy, bravery, and inner strength.

—**Patrick Dominguez**
Founder of Inner Coach

Raising My Voice is a triumph of the human spirit and the power of women to transcend the toughest obstacles. Simona Spark gives us an unflinching look at the immigrant experience, the depths of injustice and abuse and ultimately the way we can RISE despite it all. This is a story of hope delivered not a moment too soon!

—**Sara Connell**
Author, Founder of Thought Leader Academy

RAISING MY VOICE

RAISING MY VOICE

The Memoir of an Immigrant

SIMONA SPARK

PINA PUBLISHING ❦ SEATTLE

The stories and events that appear in this book are true.

Text copyright © 2021 by Simona Spark
Cover design by Simona Spark © 2021 by Simona Spark
Interior book design by © 2021 by Susan Harring

For information about special discounts for bulk purchases contact:
sales@pinapublishing.com
www.simonaspark.com
transformation@simonaspark.com

Manufactured in the United States of America
Library of Congress Cataloging-in-Publication Data Spark, Simona.

Summary:
Raising My Voice: The Memoir of an Immigrant is a true story of resilience and possibility. The lessons in this book are as diverse as author Simona Spark's life experiences. Because of her dynamic past, this memoir reaches a wide audience, and has knowledge for everyone. It provides value and guidance to those who have been subjected to domestic violence, toxic relationships, and discrimination. It sheds the light of possibility for those struggling with understanding sexuality and gender identification.

No matter who you are or where you are from, this book will remind you that you are not alone and inspire you to activate your potential. This message of acceptance and inclusivity disrupts the norms of society to invite you to live a life you desire and deserve.

ISBN:
978-1-943493-44-9 - Paperback
978-1-943493-45-6 - Hardcover
978-1-943493-46-3 - eBook
978-1-943493-47-0 - Audio Book

[1. Memoir- nonfiction. 2. Woman immigrants. 3. Immigration United States. 4. Immigration New Zealand. 5. LGBTQ parenting. 6. Single parents. 7. Abuse - relationships. 8. Interpersonal relations. 9. Self-help- nonfiction. 10. Transformation. 11. Empowerment. 12. Mind and Body- personal growth.]

To my son Andrei,

My rock, my teacher. You taught me what unconditional love is and inspire me every day to see the beauty and love in the world.

Preface

Silence kills.

I am sure you can imagine what I mean, but in this story, I will not leave you guessing. My name is Simona Spark, and I am someone willing to speak up about the silent struggles we all suffer through, and share what has happened to me. I will tell you like it is, even if it stings at first. I will say and do what there is to say and do and I will go where most won't - in conversation, and in life. I have learned to own this about myself, but it wasn't always encouraged or celebrated.

In fact, for a long time, it was the opposite. I was humiliated and shunned for having an original thought, opinion, or desire. Growing up in Communist Romania, I was constantly made to shut up, stay quiet, and suffer silently. Making 'noise' or standing out was shameful and punishable.

If being silenced doesn't physically put you in harm's way, it will certainly cause a slow death of your soul.

Being made to stay silent for the better portion of my life has had lasting effects that have required conscious healing work and years of introspection and transformation. I am sure we can all relate to some degree about how our childhoods are the reason why therapists and coaches stay in business; it is why I have a business, too. In this case, I have chosen to write this book to put the power back in your hands. As you turn these pages, you may notice the voice of your soul getting louder. I will teach you how to not only listen to it, but to put it on loudspeaker, and confidently turn that dial up as much as you wish. I will teach you how to honor and follow what you hear from within. Along with my story, there will be thought-provoking questions, reflections, and prompts for you to contemplate yourself and your life. While you learn about my experience, you can heal yours. This is a journey we will take together.

We will get acquainted very quickly throughout these pages. You can consider us friends already, and something I want to be transparent about is my own transparency. This may be a bit of a 'one-way street' situation here, seeing as you don't have the ability to share your story with me, but I want you to know that I am here for you and your evolution. We are going to talk a lot about very personal topics including abuse, traumas, trials, triumphs, and dreams. As I am sure you can understand, triumphs and dreams are very raw to share, because they too can be judged and rejected. When I chose to write this book, anxiety swept over me because I knew that I would be sharing my whole story, which meant exposing parts of my life I have never publicly shared. While my small Self would have loved to stay hidden, the urge to write this book felt more like a command from within than just some good idea. I am willing to put my Self-identity and pride aside to help you explore your own journey.

I actively worked on this book for the few years leading up to its publication, but it took me forty-four years of 'pregnancy' to deliver it into your hands. I only went into labor with this beautiful baby when I realized that the most hidden parts of my story were the ones that needed to be shared. Writing this book has been my way of going from hiding to public. I didn't always relate to speaking up or standing up for myself as 'raising my voice' until I saw it was time to share the parts of me that I have silenced. I never thought that writing a memoir could be healing, and yet, that is what I got to discover during the writing process. Unexpectedly, putting my life to paper took me deeper into healing myself.

Formally speaking, this book may be called a memoir, but it is written for you, the reader, to take a serious look at your own life and notice where you stay silent. Notice where you hide, quit, walk away, or give up. It is meant to help you notice where you tolerate the limiting and stifling behaviors of the people around you, and with that knowledge, begin to set new personal boundaries. Since we're already friends, I want you to know how I treat my people; I don't pull any punches in conversations when it means the truth will make a difference for someone. Whether you're a friend, client, family, or colleague, if we are in conversation, you are getting my truth as I see it. Because of how up front I tend to be, I am not always everyone's favorite cup of tea and I don't sprinkle in sugar just to make you feel better. I am me. I am unapologetic and I am more committed to your potential than your feelings. I'm more committed to being honest and clear than using a pretty wrapping paper that might cover the essence of what needs to be said.

That is the gift you get when talking to a woman raised in Europe, married three times, who has escaped captivity, traveled the world, and launched multiple successful careers completely from scratch. I have no time for bullshit, and any of my friends and clients will tell you, I have no problem calling anyone out on theirs. I don't believe in all the oh-so-sexy excuses you can come up with about why you can't have what you want. There is too much available to us to not live our fullest lives and contribute to each other's ascension, as well. There is no space in my world for silent suffering. I am a champion for myself, my son, and my people. I will be completely myself, as a model to inspire you to rise up.

So, while being an author is a pretty flashy title, I am going to be the Simona you would meet at a conference, at the grocery store, or on a video call. A fun, real-life fact about me: my business card has no title on it. I have worked really hard to get to the point in my life and business where I don't need a title to describe myself. I will elaborate on this later in the book. For now, I want you to know that I am going to talk to you as if we were sitting together on my couch. I am going to be real and vulnerable about my story and I am going to invite you to take an honest look in the mirror at your own willingness to be seen, heard, supported, and celebrated.

As a coach and business owner, I have made a career out of being honest with people. You, my readers, are no different. I will drop a few cuss words, make a few jokes, and deliver some hard truths about why we are stuck where we are and how we can elevate our experience of life by raising your voice. You will have a sense when this resonates with you and where in your life you can raise your voice to uplevel your experience. I call myself a 'coach' because I will go further than your friends and family when it comes to helping you reach your potential. I will do this with you the same way that I do with my clients; I will speak to your potential, not to your limitations. Some of us are blessed with people in our lives who will give it to us straight, but for the majority of my experience in America, I have observed that being polite takes precedence over being honest. I have no fear about saying what there is to say to help you move past your blocks, fears, insecurities, and limitations.

When I first stepped into the role of leader, speaker, and public figure, I never wanted my photos photoshopped. To be honest, I never wanted to be photographed at all, but over time, I became comfortable with taking and posting pictures of myself on social media and in publications. I am an 'in person' person and this has changed as I have grown. No matter what, I knew I wanted to be real, raw, and anything but fake. I wanted people to meet the woman in the picture, and not be shocked or surprised when they met me in person.

I had the same feeling when writing this book. That small and insecure Self tried to stop me from the risk of sharing pictures of my original Romanian notes and poems. Even to this day, I sometimes feel embarrassed about the broken English, the misspelled words, and the terrible grammar. When I remember where I began, my current self allows grace for that young immigrant doing her best to learn and grow.

When I first wanted to write this book in 2016, I didn't feel capable. I asked my son Andrei to help me. He was my witness. He went through all of this first-hand and I knew he could help me tell my story. He is an excellent writer, but I mostly asked him to write it because I was self-conscious about my broken English. When he wrote the first chapter as a high school freshman, it brought me to tears. I melted with admiration for what he had written; it was the story of the rose tattoo on my ankle that I got when he was four. *Four*, you guys. This child of mine eloquently recalled a memory of his mother "getting a beautiful rose tattoo to cover up an ugly time in her life" and I was blown away by his awareness and literary ability.

That first chapter was so beautiful that I kept encouraging him to help me write more. I had a brilliant plan all worked out in my head; he would write the book and I would plan our world tour. I tried to make it sound exciting, like a fun high school project for him, and instead, here I am, four years later, trying to write this book. After several failed attempts of having him write it, he finally turned to me, as brilliant and straightforward as he is, and said "mom, this is your book, your story, your experience. You're going to have to write it." I knew that to be true. We both knew that if he ever wrote a book, it would be his life, his perspective, his memories, and his lessons; not mine. I knew I'd have to figure out a way to write this book, so I started the process of getting my thoughts onto paper.

A year later, I needed to prove to myself that I could write in English. When committing to writing my first book, *No More Messy Kids* in 2018, all of those old feelings were reactivated. "I don't know English well enough. My writing sucks. Who am I to write a book? I am not good enough to..." Well, I wasn't willing to stop just because the idea of people reading my writing scared me. I knew I wanted to be an author and I definitely knew that I had a story to share. When I didn't get my memoir off the ground as quickly as I had hoped, I decided to start somewhere, anywhere, and so I wrote a smaller book to prove to my small Self that we could do big things. I had to work myself through endless nerves and self-judgment around what I still consider to be my 'broken' English.

When I finally swore to myself to write this book, it was the worst possible time in my life to take on such a large project. Between moving continents, going through the end of a marriage, living alone for the first time, going through a world-wide pandemic, and more, all signs pointed to 'wait.' Despite all of these obstacles, I knew I needed to do it.

I share this honestly, because no matter how far you climb in life, that small Self will always want to come along for the ride. Part of your job is to learn how to hear it, but not listen or take that voice into consideration. Let me give you my metaphor for this: all of the voices are welcome in my car, but I am the driver. I want to encourage everyone to chase the dreams that they consider too big or scary. It's not about telling you to go for it. It's about showing you. If I can do what I have done, you can do anything, too. If I can publish a book, you can also achieve that which intimidates you.

It is only now since I have gone through coaching, therapy, and have become a coach myself that I no longer let my fear or pride get in the way of delivering my gifts. I have received so much help and guidance in creating this book so that it can be concise, articulate, powerful, and grammatically correct! In other words, the amount of editing would make your eyeballs spin! So, when you meet me in person, you're still going to hear my thick Romanian accent, I'm going to drop a few curse words, and I will likely leave out a few correct conjunctions. So, as a woman with English as her second language, learned at the age of thirty-three, I want you to know that I had the support of friends, colleagues, and professionals to make this book what it is. There may have been many layers of meetings, conversations, and corrections, but I want to share that I poured my heart and soul into producing a wonderful, polished book for you to read today.

The same way my photos aren't changed, my words are mine. These stories, memories, and lessons are what my eyes have seen, ears have heard, and my heart has felt. I don't want to have to look or sound different in person. I want to be me because it has gotten me this far. I am also fully committed to everyone else seeing that it is okay to be themselves. Unique. Unfiltered. Uncensored. Unapologetic. You do not have to dress up, fake anything, or pretend in order to be successful. It is quite the opposite; the more *you* that you are committed to being, the more successful you have the potential of becoming.

Sure, people succeed at pretending and being fakes and con artists, but it is not sustainable. What is done in the dark always comes to light. A facade will always fall apart in due time. I know because I have tried this myself, many times. Trying to be someone or something else gets exhausting and uninspiring, and people will predictably see right through it. It is impossible for people to see you when you pretend to be someone else, so why complain about not being seen? Do you see the problem here? It is hard for others to believe us when we don't believe ourselves, so it is time to start speaking up about who we truly are. The most successful you can ever be is by discovering who you are and committing to being that and only that. You can trust that I will be me, and will always authentically show up for you the same way. I don't have to be right but I do have to be honest, so I'll speak my truth.

As I mentioned, silence kills. It kills the spirit, soul, truth, and all possibility. My life began when I started speaking up, and it took off when I started raising my voice. I will share incredible stories throughout this book about how I literally 'spoke my life' into existence and I will show you how to do the same. You have your own story to tell and you are the author of the rest of it. It's time to recognize that the pen has been in your hand all along.

I want to formally welcome you to the beginning of a beautiful journey toward your fullest, funnest, -yes, funnest. I am going to use this whole English-as-a-second-language-thing to my advantage from time to time – and finest life. I am going to ask you to quiet that small Self voice and start inviting your soul to raise its voice. Your soul will be shouting, singing, and praising by the end of our time together.

Table of Contents

Part 1

Finding Strength to Survive

Chapter 1
Speechless

I cannot recall if it was the July heat or my anticipation that made my palms sweat as I turned the key. What I do remember is hearing the echoes of my heels walking around in my new, empty, two-bedroom apartment thinking to myself, "Oh my God, I am a global citizen renting my own apartment in LA. I have a brand, an internationally downloaded podcast, a TEDx talk, and I am a leader in the LGBTQ community. This is my real life." I had all of this going on in my head, yet, I could hardly speak.

I vividly remember thinking as I turned the key to that apartment that I was officially unlocking the next phase of my life. I was opening a door to a whole new world of possibility. As I walked the bright perimeter of the apartment just taking it all in, I stopped and stood, speechless. I could feel my body tingling and tears of pride and joy welling up in my eyes as I stared out of the wall of windows overlooking the landscape of Los Angeles, revealing the mountainscape and Hollywood sign. It was like a movie scene. I remember looking out and breathing it all in; being sure to truly take in this moment. Suddenly, I had a flashback from when my life didn't look this picturesque.

I was physically staring out of a giant window, but my mind had gone back ten years prior to my first day in the women's shelter. The windows were painted black. I had not realized they were painted black; I just recognized there was absolutely no sunlight in that room. Even on a bright, sunny August afternoon the air was heavy, old, and stale. The contrast between our car ride to the shelter and walking into that old, dull building with no fresh air put a lump in my throat. I felt captive all over again. Even though they had explained to me that it was for my safety, so that my abusive husband couldn't find me, I just remember not seeing the light of day for three straight months after that. I remember feeling imprisoned when all I wanted to do was escape. I felt like I had traded one prison for another. I knew it was in our best interest but I just remember how angry I was with myself for being in this situation.

Over the phone, the shelter employee gave me very specific directions about escaping my abusive marriage. I was to arrive in a shopping center parking lot, doing my best not to be followed by my husband, and believing that someone trustworthy would pick us up and take us to safety. I had nothing else to lose. Our life couldn't get any worse than it was. I had officially gotten to the lowest point I'd ever been in my life. I hit my rock bottom. I was willing to take the risk.

I remember feeling lost after taking a two-and-a-half-hour drive in a vehicle that I had just gotten into, no questions asked, with only one bag for the both of us; myself, and my six-year-old son, Andrei. After a drive through the neighborhoods, onto the highways, back into the town again and again, I couldn't tell if we were still in Virginia or had crossed into another state. Finally, we arrived at the shelter, only to be put into complete isolation followed by a barrage of interviews to get us checked in. I had no documentation, an expired visitor's visa, no plan, knew next to no English, and had very little hope.

I landed back in my body, back in front of those clean, clear, giant windows, when I suddenly felt the warmth of the sun on my face. The heat felt like a secure hug as it brought me back into my new reality. That hug felt necessary as my logical brain took its moment to strike with panic. I heard my brain say, "starting from scratch." Suddenly, my whole body became hot and the feeling of being overwhelmed rushed in. The same way my brain chimed in, my heart spoke up, loud and clear. Right from the center of my chest, I heard, "we are different now."

As quickly as the thought of starting over took my breath away, my heart came in with a breath of fresh air. I had never bounced back so quickly, but I had noticed this was happening more often in my life these days. I was relieved by the power within when I realized I was being called to another level of healing my broken heart. I had felt that "here we go all over again," but instead, I heard my heart raise her voice louder than my mind to say that sentence, the one that kept me wanting to try. "We are different now." I really was a new woman, starting over. I was no longer that immigrant in a shelter. I was no longer that ESL student. I was no longer that young mother, scared for her son's life. I was no longer working fifteen-hour days six days a week just to make rent and buy groceries. I was no longer a woman who struggled, had to hide, or stay silent. I learned to trust myself and the fact that I could get to the other side of pain by going right through it. I was ready to deal with it this way.

I was a woman who knew it was safe to speak up. I knew I could speak out. I knew I could stand tall. I knew how to ask and go for what I wanted. I knew how to raise my voice, raise my vibe, and raise my life, and that is exactly what I was doing at this very moment. I turned to my friend Cassandra and said, "this is my new home."

How I went from a shelter with blacked-out windows to an Los Angeles high-rise, top floor apartment (affectionately known as Spark Penthouse) in a matter of ten years is something worth writing a book about. It is only through telling my story that I could possibly explain the journey my son and I have been through. It is beyond a stretch of the imagination to understand the depths I've been to, the obstacles I've overcome, and the barriers that I have busted down to be where I am today. To be able to share my story, influence millions, and make a difference on this planet feels like a duty and an honor.

In 2009, I couldn't speak English. In 2020, I raise my voice higher and louder than ever to inspire resilience and unconditional love in all beings. I have written this book to create awareness around my own story, as well as many other immigrants' journeys. Immigrant or not, I am opening up to share untold stories to open up your mind and heart to what is possible when we drop judgments, limitations, and stereotypes we hold on to and limit each other with.

It is my hope and commitment that my story will show you that if a Romanian immigrant can make it through the valleys and rise to the peaks that I have, then you can too. My request of you is faith and commitment. I will share many times throughout this book about how I continuously made declarations and dreamt of visions that I didn't always have confidence in. In fact, there were many times in my life when I could see my future but was literally too embarrassed to share it with anyone else. I would hide my notebooks and journals from other people for fear of them locking me up in an insane asylum. I had no valid reason to believe I could live such a great life, yet, here I am sitting in my top floor, LA apartment having made it to the other side of every obstacle, writing a book to tell you about it.

There is no dream too big. There is no goal too lofty. This is a conversation about you and your willingness to go for all that is possible, and we will do that together. I hope to have you see that your story matters. Your truth and gifts must be delivered so that you can raise your voice to raise the frequency of humanity and this planet. I am excited to walk with you on this new journey of introspection, self-discovery, and inspiration.

Chapter 2
Shut Up or Die

I was woken up at three a.m. by my husband, Fred, yelling, screaming, pulling the covers off, and yanking me out of bed. I was still waking up and trying to figure out what was going on when the front door shut behind both me and my son, Andrei. I remember Fred grumbling about "working so hard to pay the bills while my son and I just slept without a care in the world."

I could hardly say I didn't have a care in the world. I was constantly scared for our lives, and now, we were locked out of the house in the freezing cold in the middle of the night. It is incredible for me to think back and realize that we were captive when we were in that house, and even standing outside of it. We didn't run off or ask for help from a neighbor. In such a moment as this, I didn't know what to say, I didn't know what to do, and we had nowhere to go. The adrenaline of the situation lasted me a little, but the temperature was getting colder by the minute as we sat on the front steps.

I remember putting Andrei's feet in my pajama pockets just to keep them warm, and holding him tight. As many mothers can relate, your pain seems to go away when the priority is your child. I believe motherhood gives us superhuman strength and power. So, there we were, outside with no socks, no jackets, and paper-thin pajamas, sitting on the cold ground, freezing. The snow was as tall as the cars in the parking lot, and my bare feet were so cold on the icy sidewalk that they began to feel on fire.

Oddly enough, it was during times like these when my Romanian upbringing kicked into gear. "Shut up or die" I would hear in my head when I wanted to raise my voice and resist Fred. "Let it happen. Don't fight back. Take it. Deal with it. It's probably your fault, anyway…" These thoughts had been ringing in my head for my whole life. I was conditioned for this kind of treatment. I remember so many times in my childhood when I was not allowed to have an opinion and was threatened if I did. As the youngest of three, I was expected to do as told. When I did and if I dared to speak up, I was shut down, " You don't get to have an opinion, you are too young to talk." I learned that having an opinion and speaking my own mind was rude, inappropriate, and most importantly – dangerous.

I grew up in the countryside during Communist Romanian rule, when many areas of the country were without lights, water, and food for unforeseen stretches of time; yet, we were the lucky ones. We had land to grow our food and animals while people in the city experienced starvation and despair. There wasn't much to celebrate where I came from. Scheduled electricity time and television time, working the land, and caring for animals was what life was about. I grew up with a very strict upbringing and very little compassion or emotional connection. We didn't say "I love you" or kiss goodnight. Affection was reserved for birthdays and New Year's Eve.

Growing up in the country, we worked hard to take care of the land and animals. Dad prioritized school and grades. He had a position at the country hall and he was in charge of and responsible for the education in the village. It was understood that we were to make him proud, or better yet, not to embarrass him. We were expected to do great in school and work the land like everyone else. As the youngest, I was often left at home to care for the animals and complete other domestic tasks. While everyone was working on the land up in the hills, I would get to play around the house. I would have to sneak in playing and hide the evidence for fear of being reprimanded for having fun. For as long as I can remember, I have had to hide any joy I have ever felt.

At this point in my life, I had no joy to hide. It had been stripped away completely. My spark seemed to be suffocated and smothered out. There was no warmth within or outside of me on this particular winter morning in New Jersey. I have no idea how we survived in the cold for three hours but at about six a.m., Fred opened the front door just before the neighbors would get up and out to work and potentially see us. He finally let us in just so they wouldn't know we were out there. "Get in here so you're not seen. Don't embarrass me." He scowled as we walked back in from the freezing cold.

I really have no idea how the body functions to survive such extreme conditions. I still wonder how we did not get frostbite or freeze but we didn't. We were somehow protected. I have somehow been protected my entire life through mental, physical, and emotional lashings from the people I thought I could trust.

It is only in retrospect that I can truly see the evidence of that protection. In each trying moment of my life, I just had to rely on myself, my grit, and resilience because I had no idea how to survive each situation that I ended up in over the years. I just relied on knowing I had already survived some of the worst things people could face. I left Romania to *escape* that life, to make something of myself, to be seen as somebody different. I left to ensure that my child wouldn't grow up and turn out like most of the people I knew, myself included. I had to find another way. I thought coming to America would be that other way but now, it seemed like I walked out of my past and right back into my past of fear and hardship.

I first came to America by myself, I worked as a cashier at a gas station in Maryland and had been offered an opportunity to work in Los Angeles for the last two months of my visit, so I took it. I worked for a high-end real estate agent. My job was very simple; make her breakfast in the morning and keep her closet clean and ironed. I was amazed at how well she paid me for this, and she took me everywhere with her! Best gig ever!

Before heading off to LA, I remember my gas station manager bringing me European coffee every morning because he appreciated my hard work and effort. This meant the world to me. For the first time, I felt appreciated for my work, not for titles or a status. I was nobody in that workplace, working the night shift in the store. I was just mopping the floors and cleaning the bathroom. This was the greatest sign of appreciation that I had ever received in my life. It made such a lasting difference for me that I am writing about that daily coffee delivery here now. Every day that manager handed me a free coffee as thanks, I drank every sip with gratitude. I felt seen. I had never felt that acknowledged before and I was just ringing up people's gas and cleaning bathrooms. I kept thinking to myself, "how can I have been such a successful and accomplished woman in Romania, only to be shamed and shunned, yet, the Americans appreciate toilet scrubbers!?!" It is what sold me on getting a visa for my son and seeing the possibility of living life differently.

After three months in America, when I got back to Romania, my entire world seemed different. I was different. I couldn't unsee what I saw. I couldn't 'unfeel' what I had felt while in the States. The entire scene that I had left three months ago now felt like an alternate universe; one frozen in time where nothing ever changed. There was no going back to Romania to stay. I was going to get my son and make our way back to the U.S. I did not know what I'd be doing or how, especially with no English, but I knew that it would be different from all I had known, and that was enough for me.

When we got to America, I met Frederick and stayed with him. I found having an American love romantic. I found the whole idea of living the American dream romantic and things began moving so quickly. He made me feel extraordinary. While back in Romania, I was judged for being divorced and a single parent, here, I was admired for it. Fred made sure that he told me that over and over, and so many other compliments that I loved hearing for the first time. Within a month, we were getting married in Philadelphia. We got married in a small church with just a few witnesses, and two weeks later we had his family from Philly, New York, and Virginia come over for a weekend barbeque celebration. All his siblings, nephews and nieces were there. It was such a good time. I felt so happy and relieved to be starting my life in America on such a good foot.

Right after that weekend ended, the hell began. We lived in New Jersey and I was essentially trapped in our house. I discovered very quickly how Fred would put on this wonderful front around others, complimenting me and treating me nicely. I enjoyed the minimal times we would go out or have people over because they were my only moments of safety. The moment we were alone again, the screaming would start. He was so incredibly jealous that he would blame and accuse me of flirting and cheating and my punishment was captivity. Any time I would try to deny or argue, the fights got worse. Let me tell you something, it is really hard to stand up for yourself when you don't speak the language of your abuser. Every day was a screaming match and looked nothing like a marriage I had hoped or planned for. With no status in the US, applying for my Green Card was up to my husband and that became the daily threat over my head.

My son and I were locked in the house for days on end, forced to ration food. I remember one stretch of days, I lost count, but we were left with two cups of instant macaroni. I remembered teaching Andrei how the body can survive on water and very little food. I may have turned that experience into a math and biology lesson for him but I was just hoping my calculations weren't off. I was so scared. I was constantly scared.

I can still sense the deep internal tremble that his wrath would bring. His barking, his threats, his punishments. The sound of turning the key into the door would be enough to trigger all my fears and send me on a downward spiral of questioning everything about myself. I was afraid of his temper because he would always find a reason to snap. When I would hear that key turn, my mind would start wondering "should this be here or there? What would he want?" I would literally move things around the house just in hopes that he wouldn't find *something* to yell and fight about. The control and dominance he asserted had me doubting my ability to survive this. Knowing the accusations of cheating that would follow if I didn't pick up the phone on the first ring while he was traveling made me nauseous. I was living in a prison and he was the warden. If Fred wasn't happy for any reason, I would be in trouble with him when he got home. I could never predict how each day or night would go. I was constantly braced for impact.

Because of his insecurities, I couldn't leave the house. I couldn't connect with anybody. I couldn't have friends. I was entirely isolated. I would think, "I came to America to be free and I walked into modern-day slavery." I was spinning in the feeling of captivity and talking so much shit to myself about how I ended up in such a terrible situation. I would constantly criticize myself, "I allowed this to happen. It is my fault."

I may have been held physically captive in America. However, I was most certainly emotionally captive in Romania after my first husband broke up with me over coffee one morning after six years of dating and another eight years of marriage.

This broke my heart. He was my high school sweetheart and we practically grew up together through our relationship. I took so much risk in dating Sorin, going against my father's rules and threats. I was not allowed to date boys, but I took that chance with Sorin. Going against our very traditional upbringing, we dated young, married, and had Andrei together. I thought we had it all. I loved him so much and when we met, we would talk about supporting each other, building careers together, and having our dream life. It was definitely not considered a conventional Romanian dream life but it was ours and we were thriving together, or so I thought.

Shortly after our break-up, I found out that he had been cheating on me and many of our friends and family knew. I was so embarrassed. I felt ashamed about the situation, and what made it worse was that in light of our divorce, I was considered a disgraceful woman; a single mom, divorced, old, worthless, used.

Beyond the disgrace of being divorced at age thirty, so much of the blame was put on me. My family's and society's traditional beliefs made all of this *my* fault. I was expected to stay in the marriage and work harder to make it work. I would be told "the woman must keep the family together." I specifically remember my dad *telling* me that I couldn't divorce, that it was my job to keep the family together. The most painful judgment I received was that it was *my* fault he lost interest in me because I was gone too much for work. I was informed "a man has needs, and if a man is cheating, it must be because the woman isn't pleasing him enough to keep him around and wanting to come home."

Even at a young age, I was incredibly perceptive. This didn't feel right.

How could this be my fault? How could people not see what I saw? I was so angry, hurt, embarrassed, and confused. I also felt so alone, like no one was willing to see my side or perspective. Although I was experiencing this pain on an entirely new level, feeling like an outcast wasn't an entirely new concept to me.

I was the first twenty-two-year-old woman to apply for a position in the ING Group, insurance department, when the minimum entry age was twenty-seven. I took a huge risk even applying for the job, but knew I was capable and when I went for it, I got it. Being willing to take risks would get me where I wanted so many times in life but it didn't always make me popular amongst friends and family. I knew I was good at whatever I would put my mind to and I rose to great heights in my career, but people didn't know exactly how successful I had become. Because of the judgment, I hid my level of success due to the many negative stereotypes about successful career women. Even at the time of my early twenties in Romania, women were expected to be able to help financially by going to work, as well as tend to the family. It felt like a no win situation because being too good at a career costs your family, and only focusing on the family affected the income. This was such a hard balance to strike but it felt possible to me; until the moment my husband left me. I thought I was managing all of it well and it was our break-up that shattered my view of how it was going.

So often in my marriage and motherhood, I was encouraged to balance it all and make sure my work was going well and my husband was happy. Divorce turned that flame into a forest fire. Everyone blamed the end of our relationship on me working outside the home and it made no sense to me. "How could I be being punished for wanting my own success? Why is it *so* bad for me to want to make money, have goals of my own, and make my own name in the world?" I was made to look like I was to blame for not being able to 'keep my husband satisfied' enough to keep coming home to me. It never has made sense to me and eventually I stopped trying to understand it. It seemed like no matter how hard I tried, there was nothing I could have done different or better to make it work.

I faced another level of heartbreak when I lost many of my friends during our divorce. When I found out people knew about my husband's mistress, I figured they weren't really my friends, so I started moving on without them. It didn't feel safe enough to trust anyone with my heart. People judged, ridiculed, and shamed me for being willing to get a divorce. I was an embarrassment to my family as the first person ever within it to divorce. On top of all this pain, I had no support. I felt so isolated and instead of paying attention to it, I just began to work even more.

It was my way of coping. I was driven by the need to prove to them that I could make it on my own but it wasn't working to cover up my pain. I was hurting. This pain got worse over time, but we are proud people in Romania, mostly told to shut the tears off and get to work. When I felt that I couldn't think and didn't know what or how to feel about everything, I finally contacted a therapist.

Another limiting belief that I grew up with was that going to therapy meant you are crazy. So, I contacted this therapist and made an appointment with her in the evening. I made sure nobody would see me and even took a taxi so no one would recognize my car in her parking lot. I was so embarrassed to have been in this circumstance. Nobody was to know about this; no friend, no family, nobody! They never did, and the only way they will find out is if they ever read this.

I believe this is how I knew how to survive the isolation of my marriage to Fred. Fred was just one man. When I felt betrayed by everyone I trusted in my home country, I watched dozens of people turn their backs. Even after taking care of myself after divorce, people scoffed and scorned. At least Fred was one back that I could keep my eyes on at all times. I knew if I could escape the judgment of dozens, I could definitely escape the captivity of one. I knew I wanted out and I was going to figure out a way.

By the grace of some force greater than me, the way was made for me. I was able to leave my abusive marriage through my husband's brother. Macy didn't waste a moment alone after dinner when he quickly pulled me aside and asked me if I was okay. I could tell that he knew something was off. This made me a bit nervous at first, because he was Fred's brother, but something about the way he was paying attention put me at ease. He asked me how I was doing and I pretended nothing was wrong, but he saw a right through my answer. He didn't force me to say anything but he said as much as he could without saying a word. He very sincerely and directly told me that if I need *anything at all* to contact him. It went generally unspoken but it was very clear that he understood my situation and was willing to help me get out of it. This was the spark of hope I had been praying for.

I understood Macy's message but I did not take him up on it right away. Now, I felt a new sense of safety that I had an option. I had an escape. I was not alone anymore. I still tried to pretend that things were okay, would work out, and that I was fine. The relationship went on the same way, Fred pretended in front of others and was a monster behind closed doors. Every day after that dinner, Macy's invitation out sat in the back of my mind and yet, I still fought it. "We are in New Jersey and he is in Virginia, how can he help me? He won't help me," I thought, "after all, Fred is his brother. I am nobody."

I had finally reached my breaking point when Fred had gone on a weekend work trip four days after moving to Virginia. Andrei and I pulled in all the furniture and boxes from the garage and put the house together to be ready for when Fred came back. I remember walking around the house feeling accomplished for the first time in a long time. I had even sewed my first curtains ever, and I was so proud about how beautiful they turned out. I had made use of our time in the house and was even excited for Fred to see it completed when he got home.

I wish I could tell you that Fred walked through the door in amazement, looked at me, realized what a great wife he had, apologized, and we lived happily ever after. I think my brain might have actually thought that could have happened. Instead, he came in the door and immediately began yelling and questioning me. He asked me who helped me get everything out of the garage and refused to believe that I could have possibly put the whole house together with only my six-year-old's help. He clearly had no clue about Eastern European women and their work ethic but this was truly it for me.

I had gone above and beyond for that man. I obeyed outlandish rules and met his ridiculous expectations. I was done. There was nothing I could do to ever make that relationship work, ever make Fred happy, or ever make a good life for Andrei and myself. I had sacrificed so much of my worth, my identity, and my standards to stay in this marriage, and I got nothing but mental, emotional, and verbal abuse back. I was so fed up by being accused of cheating and I was blown away that he believed I could or would find a boyfriend in three days, in a brand new state, to help me put an entire house together. I *had been* cheated on and left in my first marriage, and I did everything I knew to do to make this one work, but I had to face what I knew was the truth; *this isn't right and this ain't it.* It was time to make our escape.

I decided to take Macy up on his offer that Monday when Fred left for work. I finally called a domestic violence 1-800 number and asked for help. I was able to organize an opportunity to stay at a women's shelter. I was still so scared of getting caught. I needed a ride. The first thing I noticed was that Macy picked us up in a different car. I already felt safer to be traveling in an unrecognizable vehicle. When we got in the car, he gave us two McDonalds lunches, one visa card with a hundred dollars on it, and twenty dollars cash. We left in a hurry with only two boxes of our stuff which Macy offered to keep in a storage unit that he had. On the drive, he gave me a small piece of paper with an address and a key to that storage unit. Unsure if it would be safe to ever see him again, he told me that I could go there without him to get our boxes if I ever needed to. This is how I would start this next chapter of my life, with no direction or status in the US, one hundred and twenty dollars to my name, and a key to a storage unit.

I will never forget that day. It was August 16th, 2010. I was simultaneously so scared of Fred finding us on our way out but felt so safe and cared for in Macy's presence. I felt protected with him, and appreciative that he would take care of us despite the fact that it was his brother who was harming us. I remember the storm of relief, gratitude, fear, urgency, and finality that was stirring within me. I could hardly catch my breath the entire time. It seemed as quickly as we had left the house, we had arrived at the supermarket parking lot. I did my best to express my gratitude to Macy but I wasn't sure if it would ever feel like enough to match how I felt. We said our goodbyes and he left us.

Macy's generosity taught me something powerful that day: in spite of blood relations, people do the right things at the right times. I had not seen or believed that concept much from my past, but his act of generosity opened up a new world in my physical reality and my mind. I do believe that good things happen to good people, and this was when I finally started to see the glimmers of hope that would lead us to the rest of our lives.

As big of a risk as it felt, the reward seemed even bigger. Our freedom, our safety, and our ability to live the real American dream were on the line, and I was willing to take a leap of faith out of that marriage no matter where I landed. Being happy, healthy, well, and prosperous was still a possibility to me and I was willing to find out how to make that dream happen. I just knew and finally accepted that it could have never happened in that marriage and I was finally ready to leave. For the first time, I felt the new belief sinking in that no man can decide my future, no one could decide my future. No one but me.

Chapter 3

Breaking the Silence

I had made it out of that marriage but I was not in the clear yet. I had made it out of the isolation but I was still not out of captivity. I took the chance to escape Fred's rules but I had stepped into a new set of rules. This felt like being transferred prisons. I went from locked doors to blackout windows. The darkness I felt was both within and outside of myself. Hope may have been sparked by Macy's help, but that flame was weak.

I was not allowed to leave that shelter building for three months. Three months of stagnant, dull air, and twice a week therapy that made me cringe. I couldn't stand the idea of having to go to therapy where Miss Anne, the art therapist, would encourage me to share my experience. The assignments between sessions were to draw and write. In the session, the invitation was to speak and share what I was feeling. She would ask me to draw something or come up with some form of expression to share my thoughts, feelings, and emotions. No matter how many times she'd ask me how I felt or invite me to talk about anything, I would just sit there watching the clock on the wall, waitting for the session to be over. I hated being forced to go to those sessions. I didn't want to speak. I couldn't speak. I had no words for what I was going through, so I stood in silence. I felt embarrassed, small, and scared, but I wouldn't share that not with her, not with anyone.

For my entire life, I was not allowed to speak up. I learned in school at a very young age that if and when you are allowed to speak, it better be the right answer. There was such an expectation and pressure to be perfect. I had no answers or anything perfect to say, I was lost. I had to silence my feelings and repress them in order to survive. All too often, even into my adulthood, I have been getting in trouble for having feelings, and have been told to shut up and threatened for crying or complaining. It's really all I have known for as long as I've known.

Now, here I was, in a therapist's office at a women's shelter being encouraged to talk about what was going on within me. I had to shut my feelings down for so long that even with permission to feel and share, I didn't seem to have access to them. To attempt to communicate any of that seemed pointless. I only knew how to numb myself to survive. Trying to awaken those pathways in my head and heart was just not available to me.

Ms. Anne would ask me question after question and I couldn't come up with any answers. I was continuously encouraged to draw or paint. I could not come up with anything and I couldn't even pretend. I just sat there silent, session after session.

I was definitely less concerned with my own life and therapy and more concerned about my son. Beyond that, I was interested in getting out of this new prison. I couldn't stand being trapped in this building any longer. I was always looking for a way out but the most terrifying part of it was that I had nowhere to go. There seemed to be no options out there for us. I feared how long we would have to stay there. No one could tell me when we would be able to leave. It felt like time had stopped just for us while

I watched other women coming in every day, leaving shortly after with a concrete plan in their hands.

It wasn't until later that I was able to start going to the local library. Since it was the only place I could go, I would go every day while Andrei was in school. It was my temporary escape. For the first time, I picked up a self-help book, and it changed my life! I learned that I have the power to change my life, or so it said in those books. I didn't believe it but I wanted it to be true. It was through those books that I learned it is safe to dream and have dreams. For a time, those personal development books became my escape. I would read inspiring stories of leaders who rose up out of their own personal hell. This inspired me to keep dreaming when everything in my life continuously felt dull and hopeless.

Our expired documents were a big cause of what kept me feeling hopeless. It was legal for me to be in the US because I was married to a US citizen, but with no status, I had no authorization for work. We were simply not in the system and we couldn't access any government programs that support families in these circumstances. This was a terrible and limiting experience. The idea of moving forward with no documentation seemed like a challenge equivalent to climbing Mount Everest with no training. I had no idea where to start, except for at that library. I began to educate myself and connect with others as much as possible.

Before we go on any further in this memoir, it's time for an 'Immigration 101' class. This may seem silly, *and* it is only through my first-hand experience that I know exactly how unclear so many people are about the immigration process. I, too, was very unclear about it when I first arrived here. It was my research at the library that helped me figure out what I could possibly do to start helping myself. So before I keep just telling you 'Visa this' and 'authorization that,' explaining a few of these details early on will make it easier to follow along on my journey. Not just mine, though. The subtitle of this book is *The Memoir of an Immigrant*.

I am not the first or the last. This story isn't one-of-a-kind. It is the story of so many, and I am just giving you my version, my experience of being in nerve-wracking, unknown territory. So while you read about Fred or Andrei or Miss Anne, keep in mind that these are just the names in my life. It could be anyone. Much of what I have faced is what countless others have experienced as well: your neighbor, your brother-in-law, your employee, your friend, and so many more.

Immigration is a long, complicated process that gets messy and confusing. The best I can do for you is lay out a few of the facts, figures, and explanations; which I will do in a moment. I enjoy helping people who have never been exposed to the immigration process gain a better perspective of what we go through to earn our right to visit, stay, work, vote, and integrate into this great country. It is a major goal of mine to communicate to those unfamiliar with what immigrants go through and especially those who may have a misunderstanding of why so many people from other countries come to make the United States their refuge. I am proud to raise my voice for those who never feel heard, seen, or understood in a land they love so much.

Before I dive into the details, I feel especially inspired to let you into the heart of an immigrant. Often, even just thinking or talking about freedom brings me to tears. I have written a whole book and yet, there isn't any perfect set of words I can put together that can explain the deep sense of gratitude, pride, and joy my freedom brings me. Even using those descriptions don't seem to serve justice to the way I feel about what I have gone through to get where I am today.

When I think back, the most American pride that I ever recall feeling was the first time I got to vote. As soon I got into the parking garage and saw the tables dressed with American flags, I started crying. I couldn't stop. People kept walking to me asking, "Are you okay? Do you need anything? Can we call someone?" I was okay. I was happy! I was free! I was about to vote for the first time as a US Citizen and I had no idea that this is how I would feel.

I walked slowly, moving from table to table to sort out my registration, and made my way into the booth. My heart was racing the whole time and before I knew it, I had voted! I walked out and sat on a bench in the beautiful garden of Beverly Hills City Hall and cried. I had the past ten years passing through my body; the ups and downs, the struggle, all of it. I was overwhelmed with gratitude and joy. Freedom took on a new meaning for me. For the past decade, I was working and paying taxes like any other American but did not have the right to vote, not until that day. I had never felt so equal in my life. That day that changed me forever.

It is not exactly freedom itself, but the *essence* of freedom that leaves me speechless. Every Fourth of July is so special to me because of what it represents. I have American pride that inspired me to walk my way fully through the complicated immigration process and earn my right to vote in this country. What I am clear about is that my voice matters and I am a contribution to this country. No matter how long it took to acquire my citizenship, I was granted the freedom to pursue it, and so I did. *That* is the beauty and power of the age-old saying, "life, liberty, and the pursuit of happiness."

As US citizens, we have so many choices. I feel limitless here. I get to lead an amazing life filled with possibility and expansion. The choice to live here and my persistence to stay here weren't just for me, of course. I have had the incredible gift of raising my son with authenticity, possibility, and courage. As I will share more in this book, I am brought to more tears that my son, who came out as homosexual at the age of fourteen, gets to lead a life free from harm, discrimination, judgment, and limitation. Witnessing how safe he feels coming out to me and to live free inspires me everyday.

I have noticed how many Americans do not fully grasp the dangers that exist in other countries, but I will never take our safety on American soil for granted. Even at times when we didn't have documentation, we were still cared for by kind Americans and supported to get on our feet. A new paradigm shift that changed me forever was getting help from people who volunteered to help us, for free; as in *not* paid to do so. This was astonishing to me because it was a non-existent idea in my country. It took me some extra time to trust people for just caring for us and loving us without asking for something in return.

It is simply incomparable to what people in other countries face. Even at a young age, Andrei also has a healthy understanding and respect of freedom because he witnessed my journey in earning my liberties. He has his own liberation journey in his own right. We get to live free from fear and we get to choose, dictate, and create the quality and direction of our lives. We get to have our own opinions, values, desires without life-threatening consequences. I value nothing more than I do freedom.

Sometimes my tears are those of appreciation, and sometimes, they are tears of sadness to see so many native-born Americans who do not get to experience a different point of reference for exactly how blessed they are. This is a great, big world, much of which I have now seen, and I still love to call America home. The opportunities and freedoms are endless here.

Okay, immigration class is officially in session. Grab your notebooks if you need and when this is all over, I invite you to get to know an immigrant on a much deeper level than "where do you come from and why did you come here?" It may be your best conversation starter but consider that it is everyone's. It is tiring to be asked this question daily, even multiple times per day. If I had a dollar for every time I have been asked, "You have an accent, where are you from?" I would never have to work again. When working in retail, let me tell you, it got so tiring! I'm not saying that people are not genuinely curious, but maybe next time, consider that you are not the first to ask, you might be the twentieth person to ask that very same day. An invitation would be to check in with yourself "why do I ask?" before automatically using that question to strike up a conversation. In my own, and many others' experiences, this can be a real trigger for immigrants. While we appreciate your interest, maybe spice it up a little in conversation. You may learn more than where we are from and this can open up a whole new world of possibility.

No matter how you start an interaction, I am calling you to be someone who makes outsiders feel welcome and makes immigrants feel like the brothers and sisters that we are. No matter where we come from, we have hearts that feel, minds that think, and ears that hear. No matter what language we speak, we all speak the language of love. So, find out more about the people around you and open your heart and mind to a new perspective.

To my fellow immigrants, this book is a dedication to your journey. It is your reminder that you can achieve anything you can envision and to never quit on your dreams. You have every right to your freedom and to thrive. Believe in what's possible and go for it boldly. I will share everything I know to help pave your path toward your greatest desires. Keep going for your dreams, ask for help when you need it, and allow your fellow Americans to witness your journey. It is up to us to normalize this process and close the gap between immigrants and born citizens. As I said a moment ago, we are all brothers and sisters no matter our origin or destination. It is time we lock arms in our journey forward.

You have no idea how many times I have had to have the immigration process explained to me. I can't even tell you how many times that might have been because I've lost count. It is at least ten times the number of instances I've had to explain it to someone else, I can say that much. I know I am about to give you the Professor Spark version but there really should be a class on this shit. I mean, seriously! How is this not a more common conversation in today's world? Okay, now here is my simplest breakdown.

There are different types of visas. Having your visa is a status. It gives you specific rights in this country. A tourist visa gives you the right to visit and a work visa gives you the right to work. You must apply and renew visas frequently and there many different variations of how long visas can last. When you enter or re-enter the country, you get a new visa that determines how long you are allowed to visit. Through the beginning of this process, an immigrant receives an 'alien number.' We *have* to change the name of this! It is so triggering for many immigrants, as most of us experienced being treated as aliens during the process; as if we don't belong here. To have the right to live in this country, you need a permanent resident visa; also known as a 'green card.' We do eventually get a social security number when we obtain our green card, so we eventually become free from our alien number, but the name of that number never feels good.

Many immigrants only ever become residents. A resident has all of the rights of an American citizen except for one: the right to vote. An immigrant who becomes an American Citizen has the right to vote. To me, it was such a great honor to reach this immigrant status. As can be said for so many achievements in life, the journey was just as special as arriving at the destination.

There are a few different ways to acquire your residency. You can win the lottery. How this works is every year the USA grants a specific amount of "free" green cards to certain countries. The chances of winning feels like the likelihood of winning the cash lottery in the United States: one in a million. Another option is that specialized employment can pay for and facilitate the process. In other words, if you are an expert in your field and a company wants you working in their country, they can apply for your green card and expedite the process for the sake of your services in their country.

Another option is to marry a US citizen. This is the easiest and fastest way to get a green card, and can be the most troublesome, as a lot of fraud is committed within that system. Because of this, the application is analyzed under the assumption that it is a "fake" marriage for the sake of citizenship. The other way this can be challenging is that the American must apply for the Visa on the immigrant's behalf. This is the trouble I ran into in my marriage. An immigrant cannot apply for themselves, so this meant that Fred had control over my life: my status, and my ability to stay in the country were in his hands. Because he would punish me by not applying, I was trapped in my marriage for fear of being deported and sent back to a life I never planned on returning to. This was a different level of codependency. He used the application as a threat as well as a token for making peace after a fight. I felt owned by him.

Please pay attention to this: there were *so* many cases of immigrants being abused by a US family member, just like me, that they had to come up with a special visa for these immigrants: VAWA - Violence Against Women Act. This is alarming! I *wish* my story was unique and it's not. More people need to know about these statistics and I want to share that this option is not just for women, it is also for men, children, or parents of US lawful permanent residents or citizens. I learned about this option while in the shelter and it is what gave me an option to have a better life. Without the shelter volunteers' help, I may have never known. I want to tell you in case this knowledge can help someone else along the way.

It is not illegal to be in the country after the visiting time frame has expired, as long as you are married to a US citizen or have become a green card holder. You have the right to stay but you have no right to work, pay taxes, drive, or vote, and ultimately, this is so limiting that it doesn't really feel like living. In my relationship, it felt like modern day slavery. Our relationship had abuse of many types and one of them was the leveraging of my status. It was degrading and made me feel less than human. When it did come time to apply for my status after leaving my marriage, there were so many layers of difficulty of proving mental and emotional abuse to obtain permission to apply for my status on my own, that I consider it a miracle. I will share that experience in just a few pages.

So, thank you for coming to my now second TED talk. I will always get on my immigration education podium whenever I find the opportunity to. I would say that "class is dismissed," but for the duration of this book, you will continue to learn more about the challenges, barriers, and obstacles one must face to become an American citizen. And now, back to our regularly scheduled programming...

Because I couldn't work without documentation during my time in the shelter, I became a volunteer at the library. This gave me access to research and email, which was my only chance to connect with the outside world. This would become my saving grace over time.

Being able to go to the library and talk to other people began to help me find words and feelings again. I was still in hiding, my email was shut down, my Facebook account closed, and I couldn't tell anyone that I was in the shelter. Sharing the address was definitely out of the question, for safety reasons, of course. I certainly wouldn't say I was singing and dancing through the halls of the shelter, but reading those books sparked something in me. It helped me learn more English, and this grew my confidence slowly and subtly. I didn't really know the effect this was having on me until one day, Miss Anne handed me a notebook. It was this thin, spiral-bound, elementary school notebook for a young girl. It was yellow with purple flowers. I didn't think much of it at first so I just took it from her and kept it with me.

That same day, I needed to go to Macy's storage unit to find something in my two boxes that I was looking for. I don't know what it was, but I do remember every second of that experience. As soon as I unlocked that storage door, I had that ice-up-my-spine feeling. It was dark, cold, and smelled like dry dirt. There was no electricity in this small space that was too big for my two boxes. Opening those boxes opened the floodgates within me. I saw the mess that was my life represented inside of those two boxes. I sat there, staring at that mess, and feeling a storm brewing in my heart. I was so overwhelmed at what my life had been reduced to and I was also so moved that I sat there, opened up the notebook that Miss Anne gave me, and wrote my first English poem, *How I Live is Who I Am*.

I poured my heart out onto the pages of that notebook and was finally able to find the words that Miss Anne had been waiting for in our sessions. I couldn't draw it in a picture but I could put it down in words. Although my English was still very underdeveloped and unrefined, I decided to commit to English. This was my new country, so I became willing to accept it as my new language. Even though it may have not made sense to anybody else, I was able to put this poem together in a way that made sense to me, in a way that truly expressed how I felt staring into those heaps of my belongings in those two boxes. I was so ready to begin my transformation toward my liberation. I let my heart move the pen on that paper. This was my very first step of declaring and facing where I am; accepting my current reality.

When I took my journal back to therapy and showed Miss Anne, she read page after page, flooded in tears. I laugh as I think about it now but I remember saying to myself, "What do I need therapy for? I'm not the one crying, you're crying. I don't need therapy, you do!"

Miss Anne was so proud and excited to finally hear some of my self-expression and she encouraged me to write more. I did write more. I wrote seven poems that I will share throughout this book that got me through some of the darkest parts of my journey. All of this writing inspired me to start dreaming, visioning, and imagining. I wrote my poems and visions on flash cards and in a little diary that I still have to this day.

Even now, when I go back and read those poems, I am simply astonished. I don't know *who* wrote those poems. They feel as if I had channeled them, because all I can remember is how broken I felt. I wonder how I could have possibly put these words together the way that I did at the time that I did. It is as if I was taken over by a force greater than myself to deliver a message to the broken, tired, worn-out, hopeless version of me at a time that I needed it most. I was my best encouragement and these poems got me through a deep, long valley of pain.

I will share these poems throughout the book in correlation with my journey and evolution. As I have mentioned, I knew it was time to write this book when I realized there were parts of me that I was hiding and withholding. These poems and the accuracy of my visions still freak me out. I had always hidden them for fear of being considered crazy. It is only in recent years, that I have become more willing to share *so* openly. To be transparent, it took some inner work to be willing to expose these poems. They are very personal to my journey. I adjusted them slightly from their original wording in order for them to make sense because they were written at such an early stage of learning English. I hope that my willingness to be seen for the naturally imperfect being that I know I am will inspire others to raise their voices, as well. You will read a few more poems as this book goes on but it was this poem that opened my heart and the floodgates of feeling again.

How I Live is Who I Am

I have this heavy thought
About how others might see me
Through the way my things are set
Is showing out my feelings
I'm looking to myself
I'm living in a shelter
And all the things I own
Are mixed up in two boxes

Are all in this storage
That doesn't have a light
But all of my belongings
Are safe behind the lock
And so am I in here
In just one single room
There is no danger near
I'm finally safe, is true

When I open up the boxes
And saw all that big mess
I realized and faced it
Are as my thoughts in my head
I need to put some order
Through all my little things
So I can see more clear
And find whatever needs.

You might say "Are just stuff"
But they are more than this
Are all I have to start
To build my life, my dreams
The place I'm living now
Is not where I want to be
But this is the perfect spot
To take me to my dream

I have to clean the storage
And dust all my stuff
And organize in here
I have to, it's a must
The same work has to be done
With all my mismatched thoughts
I want to think clear now
No longer can be lost

I know, that day is coming
Whenever I'll be ready
To take all my belongings
And place them properly
In my own cozy place
They will be all I need
My mind will be relaxed
Happy, just living the dream.

It wasn't just poetry that saved me. Remember that miracle I mentioned earlier? Once I began my immigration process, I started with no

documentation and had zero proof of mental, emotional, and verbal abuse. I wasn't sure how to go about where to start or how to explain my situation. I felt very stranded trying to establish my legal status and identity in the United States.

In order to be able to leave the shelter, I also needed to be able to stand on my own. This felt impossible without a legal status and the right to work. That is when I was introduced to the VAWA application. I was so tough on myself at this phase of my life. This was not how I imagined coming to America. It was not how I imagined getting my US documentation. It was not how I imagined starting our life here. I never planned on needing a VAWA application to acquire my citizenship. I wanted to be able to become an American citizen on much more noble terms and I struggled with so many feelings of worthlessness about the whole process. I was once again feeling embarrassed, humiliated, and ashamed about the reality I was living, and my life came down to this option. I had to work through my own self-criticism to truly allow myself the opportunity to stand on my own two feet and start the life we wanted here, on our own.

Without legal papers, I could not work, rent, or live on my own. It was time to give up my self-criticism and distorted sense of pride and start the process. Part of that application was getting proof or letters of support that I was actually struggling with domestic violence in my marriage. Can you imagine how hard, close to impossible, it is to prove emotional abuse? It was explained to me that all I can do is collect letters from friends and family members. "What friends?" I thought fearfully, "What family members? Even if I would have these people, they would never know what went on behind closed doors."

I was so afraid it wouldn't work because emotional abuse doesn't happen in public, it's always kept hidden. I asked anyway, but I wasn't sure the letters would be enough. I was able to get two letters; one from a neighbor friend whose child I babysat a few times, and one from an ESL class colleague that I barely knew, since I was not allowed to go to the classes for too long. All I had were two people. Two people who didn't know what was happening in my house, that's it. It felt so hopeless. I knew in my heart that if I really wanted to 'prove' emotional abuse, I needed to get a letter from Macy. I knew it was time to meet up and ask him in person for this kind of help. When I asked for his support, he was happy to do whatever he could to help me get out, get up, and get going.

What I found out in talking to him that time was that Fred had a previous marriage in which he had done the same thing to his first wife that he had done to Andrei and I. He had a history of abuse and his brother knew it. I am so glad he was willing to help any woman get out of that situation. He wrote me a letter of support revealing enough information for me to qualify for my Visa through VAWA. This finally began the process of gaining my life back.

I am forever grateful for Macy's willingness to go beyond blood to do what he knows is right for a fellow human or his 'sis,' as he calls me to this day. It restored my faith in my future and myself. He may have written it but I was proud of myself for taking the chance to ask for his support. I finally learned how to ask for help. I was noticing how raising my voice and my hand to ask for support was what was saving me from tragic situations. I was learning how to use my words more powerfully every single day. Poetry might have kept me going during my time in the shelter, but in terms of writing, Macy's testimony was the piece of writing that truly saved me.

Quite frankly, being a US Citizen in and of itself is a miracle and a blessing that I refuse to take for granted. That process has shaped, refined, and redefined who I know myself to be. It has stretched me beyond recognition, and now, I stand on a firm foundation of self-awareness after having been forced to prove myself for eight consecutive years. It changed my whole identity. It changed my identity so much that my name change soon followed. When you become a US citizen, you get the opportunity to choose your name! So, I did. I chose a name that aligns with who I am now. I am Simona freakin' Spark, and I am an American Citizen.

Chapter 4

Breathless

While working as a volunteer at the library, having access to the computers, I was able to connect with an old friend from Romania, Tatiana, who now lived in Minnesota. This gave me a bridge out of the shelter and into a new life. I accepted Tatiana's kind and open-hearted invitation to stay at her house until I got on my feet, and that's exactly what I did.

Andrei and I packed up our one bag, I got my boxes from Macey's storage unit and away we went. It was a long train ride from Richmond, VA to Chicago, IL, and from there, another train ride to Winona, MN. We went from a snowless winter in Virginia to freezing cold and a snow-taller-than-cars kind of winter in Minnesota. Making our way back into 'the real world' was a bit of an adjustment but I could feel my frequency rising with each move. I couldn't say I felt super independent, but at least I wasn't completely reliant on a man I couldn't trust or a shelter staff with rules that I didn't completely understand that suffocated me. After a few months of staying with my friend and her family, Andrei and I were able to start living a more normal life, but still without an immigration status, yet.

Flash forward and I was starting to get my feet back on the ground. I was working so hard that I quite literally forgot to take care of myself. I was now working at a high-end optical shop located under the Mayo clinic in Minnesota and doing everything I knew to do to give us a good life. That included working nonstop to make rent and groceries. I had been trying so hard to make it on my own that one day, I was struggling just to breathe. I found myself in the back room of the store with no strength to scream for help. I couldn't breathe.

After some chest pain and shortness of breath, I was rushed to the hospital where I was informed that my symptoms matched a heart attack. I was instructed to be supervised and run blood work every four hours to confirm I would be okay. I was so scared. It was the middle of the day and I was working nonstop. I didn't have time to stop. The idea of being in the hospital and out of work only panicked me more and made it even harder to breathe.

Not only was I worried about my health and all of the thoughts about what was going to happen with Andrei, I was also panicking about the medical bill. My thoughts were racing, which didn't help my heart. I kept trying to figure out how to get out of here in time to pick up Andrei from school. My boss, Tammie, assured me that everything was going to be okay, and that she would cover the hospital expenses. This was such a huge help and relief. She also organized a colleague that Andrei knew to pick him up from school. The support I felt made the pain in my chest slowly subside. Four hours and another set of tests later, I got all of my testing done, and got my answers.

They informed me that it was acid reflux, and taught me that acid reflux is usually activated by high stress and anxiety. When they discovered it was acid reflux, the doctor sat down and visited with me, "where is your stress coming from these days?" he asked pretty plainly.

All I thought was, "where *isn't* my stress coming from these days?!?"

I was a single mom, now working Monday through Saturday. Andrei was always the first to be dropped off at school in the morning and the last to be picked up late from the after school program. I would use Sunday to attempt to catch up on everything from throughout the week: laundry, cooking, grocery shopping, all of the domestic tasks. It was all on me, no help, no delegating. I was absolutely exhausting myself. There was no time to care about how I felt because I was not willing to fail at giving my son and I a great life and a chance to succeed independently. I did not want to lose any of the progress or momentum I had been working so hard on making.

There was never really a time of stopping for me. In attempting to live a normal life, I had started a new relationship and ended it quickly when I knew he wasn't the right guy. Although I was more independent and determined, ending a relationship at this time had probably sent me over the edge of my health.

I was tired, worn out, struggling, and my body was starting to fall apart, too. It was as if I was getting the message to sit down, relax, and cool it, but I simply didn't know how to. I was so afraid of falling behind that I did everything I could to stay up and stay ahead. Pausing or slowing down for me meant giving up or failing, and that just wasn't an option for me. I wasn't willing to give up, but truthfully, ending up in the hospital is when I knew I needed to make a change, or a few.

I did start to make a change. I started to take a bit more care of myself, get some more rest, and become more mindful of my health and wellbeing. I started being more self-sufficient but I also took a break from trying to do it all and be it all. I began to relax a little bit when I gave myself permission to be my own woman. I decided to swear off dating for a while and start falling in love with myself. Then, I recognized that I was no longer letting other people tell me how to live my life. I began noticing what people I needed to 'break up with' in order to hear and listen to my own thoughts and my own desires regarding my life. This became a game changer for me. I was starting to hear my own intuition and feel really good about it. This is when I began to set new personal boundaries with friends and family members. When I did this, a lot opened up for me. Making that change made all of the difference in my life.

In fact, working myself into absolute exhaustion used to take my breath away in a physical sense, but now, it is my dream come true that my life is what takes my breath away.

Flash forward seven years from living in those apartments in snowy Minnesota, to leaving dinner with husband number three, my son, and his boyfriend in New Zealand. With a full belly and heart, the warm breeze wrapped me up like a hug as we walked to the game room for some family fun. I stopped to take in a full breath of that warm air and I found myself already ten feet behind my son and his boyfriend, hardly able to take another step forward. Dean stopped next to me and we just watched those two young men in love.

When I looked up, that warm air got caught in my throat. Almost like the day I felt like I was having a heart attack, I had this moment of breathlessness. My chest was aching but it wasn't painful this time; it was expansive. I seriously felt as if my heart were bursting from pride, joy, love, and complete awe of what our life had become.

As I lagged behind my Andrei and his boyfriend, I began crying tears of gratitude. Just standing there, weak in the knees, I was smiling, crying, and laughing all at the same time, I simply asked, "do you *see* this?!?"

Between my crying and gasping for my next breath, I was able to spill out "Don't you see this beautiful scene? My son is able to love his boyfriend in public. We are able to have a family dinner without fear or ridicule. We get to have a loving relationship, even if we are not together anymore. This could never be true if I never left Romania. Our life is just so amazing and I am so grateful."

I couldn't stop the tears and I didn't care to, either. I was so overjoyed by the blessing of life in this moment that I was willing to be a blubbering mess in the middle of the street. My heart was overflowing with astonishment and appreciation. I am tearing up a bit even as I write this now as I recall the times in the shelter when not only could I not express my emotions, I couldn't even feel them. Being able to feel the full range of emotions has made my life so rich with vibrant experiences. Knowing what I came from and what I have gone through, I just melt at what has transpired over the last decade to manifest into such a beautiful scene full of love, acceptance, life, and endless possibility.

So instead of brushing it off and hurrying on, I walked slowly, taking it all in, and continued to cry and smile as wide as I possibly could. We were lucky to have a very special moment of acknowledging all the blessings in our lives. It was as if for that moment, nothing but pure love existed.

In more recent years, I am surrounded by a reality I could have never imagined. No, seriously. My thirty year-old, Romanian-roots-self could not have even made up a crazier story about what my life currently is. Even if she had been told about it, she would have laughed at the idea of it all. My current life never even occurred to that version of me, but I am sure glad she had no clue what she was getting into. She may have tried to do things differently and at this point in my life, I understand how every event has played an important role in where I am today. I have far surpassed the dreams written down in notebooks, diaries, and on flashcards.

I am living a life I never could have imagined. It is something so great and beyond what I could have created alone. It is the divine intervention of so many co-creative components that have driven my life here, there, and everywhere to have arrived on that evening walk from dinner to the game room, melting over the beauty of life and love.

When I sit back in the stillness to meditate and reflect, I can still hardly breathe. I am consistently astonished by what I've created. How could I have possibly ended up where I am? How could I have ended up in a completely opposite situation from what I grew up in?

I grew up in an old-fashioned, strict, Romanian upbringing full of limitations, restrictions, anger, frustration, yelling, fighting, and aggression. Now I live, work, succeed, and thrive in an industry of openness, acceptance, abundance, love, inclusion, no labels, no judgments, caring, affection, compassion, and plenty more. I could have hardly dreamt this up years ago. Growing up in a reality of being threatened to be beaten for dating or even kissing a boy, it never occurred to me that my future held a reality in which I would be getting text pictures from my seventeen-year-old gay son, kissing his boyfriend, FaceTiming me to show me the romantic space they reserved for their one month anniversary. It really blows my mind.

There are days that I fall to my knees in praise for the ways I have been saved, protected, guided, and led through life. I am so grateful for the valleys I've been through and the peaks I have visited. I am so happy to be where I am and will never forget where I came from. I am often short for words to truly express my amazement with the reality I have lived within an eleven-year gap.

It truly takes my breath away to stand at some of the peaks of life and see what's on the horizon. It is an out-of-body experience to turn around and see what was in my past and how I have risen above it all. The barriers that used to feel like mountains look like speed bumps from where I now stand in life; all because I became willing to raise my voice, take a stand for myself, and follow through on the vision that I can so clearly see in my mind's eye.

I get to have this life because I never gave up on myself. I never gave up on the promise of the American dream. I now get to enjoy being a global citizen because I was willing to break down my own borders and barriers. I was willing to take down the walls around my heart and receive the grace of a higher power within me and through me to truly create amazing things far beyond anything I could have comprehended or dreamt up over a decade ago.

I thank myself. I thank my son. I thank my Earth Angels. I thank all the powers that be for moving me through the spaces that have gotten me to where I am today. Throughout the rest of this book, I am going to share more directly with you about how *you* can do this, too. I am going to shift this story from me, myself, and I to yours, yourself, and you, and how you can overcome everything by raising your voice and your vibration.

I am going to help you find your own way. I am going to pave the path and shine light down it so that you may walk boldly into your imagined future.

I live a life of possibilities and expansions, with paradox still being part of this lifestyle. I believe we are great as we are and always have room to grow. While I'm still learning this language, I'm very intentional about enhancing my vocabulary. Many of my clients know me for 'firing' a few English words right out of our vocabulary. They know that once I have fired a word, they can no longer use it with or around me; it no longer exists to me. One of those words is 'challenge.' I have taken the word challenge out of my vocabulary because I believe that calling something a challenge is just a sexy excuse not to demolish it with your power and will.

I do not believe in a challenge being a roadblock that sends you packing up and heading home. A challenge is a fire to walk through; the fire singes away everything that is not you so that you may become everything that you are meant to be. More than that, with each word that I fire, we get to creatively come up with new solutions for going through it. At each stage of life, we approach a new fire that will shape us more honestly into our boldest, strongest, most original selves. No bullshit can withstand the fire of truth. So from here on out, the word challenge is fired.

You are *not* limited. You are *not* without. You are *not* incapable.

You have everything you need and more to create an incredible and an extraordinary life.

Living a life that takes your breath away takes vision, grit, determination, and commitment. It takes willingness to exceed all personal expectations and release every excuse that would stop you on your way.

I have lived every 'challenge' I can imagine an immigrant might face in attempting to create their best life. I am willing to pour my heart into this book to fill yours up with faith, hope, and inspiration to go forward. I am excited to walk this journey with you. Let's begin.

Paper Never Forgets!

Write down your insights.

Part 2

The Breaking Points

Chapter 5
Time to Face Deportation

I imagine that throughout the first portion of this book, you may have been able to relate to a few of my stories and memories. No matter where you come from, how you were raised, or where you think you are headed, life tends to hand us similar trials to test and strengthen us along the way. Whether your experience of life has been similar, parallel, or vastly different, many of us have faced soul-crushing defeats, seemingly bottomless pits, and fearful dead-ends that seemed to be the end of our story. I also imagine that if you have gotten this far into the book that you can relate to something, if not many things, that I have already shared.

In this second part of the book, I am going to share a lot about anger, resentment, frustration, and defeat, to ultimately tell you that there is life beyond our breaking points. So much is possible, even the possibility to thrive beyond our disappointments. Just past our breakdowns await our breakthroughs and successes if we just have the faith, grit, and resilience to keep going further than what scares and stops us.

When I planned out this book and decided to talk about anger, I had to really ask myself, what is anger? I looked up all kinds of definitions. I liked some and not others and it came down to what anger is for me. Anger is an open door to healing. I look back at my life and can find all the trauma stored in my body. As I became willing to look at all that trauma, I was surprised by a question that arose; how come I feel so much shame for things I did not do, for things that have been done to me? I believe that shame comes up through the anger door. So, for me, the root of my anger is shame. I invite you to look for yourself, what is anger for you?

At many points in my life, I have blamed, shamed, and hated other people, but primarily, I have done so to myself. I have doubted, questioned, and cried time and time again about how life could get as bad as it had and how I could let myself end up in such terrible situations. In this section, I will explain how I made it through the most trying times and walk you through my process of moving through anger, pain, and confusion. I will explain how I took responsibility for the quality and direction of my life, with the intention of helping you identify your own process.

We have many breaking points, and one of mine was after that 3:00 a.m. fight when Fred sent Andrei and I out into the cold, in our pajamas, to sit outside until dawn. I remember sitting out there absolutely freezing to the bone, going numb physically, mentally, and emotionally. It was a new all-time low for me. I knew our lives couldn't get any worse. I knew this was it for me. I would do whatever it took to get help. I was ready to get out of the relationship and because I had no friends and nowhere to go, this meant going to the police for help. This also meant I was willing to face deportation.

That next morning, I told Fred I was going to the police. I told him what we have is beyond repair and that I was not willing to be treated that way. I had tolerated so much and my limit had been surpassed. There was nothing else he could do to me that would be worse than turning myself in and being sent back to Romania. I had hit the bottom. I couldn't go any lower than this. I was willing to risk it all and lose it all just to save our lives and my sanity.

When I told him I'd be leaving, he apologized and begged me to stay. He tried to be sweet and kind and make up for it and worst of all, it worked. He printed out the form for applying to my immigration status and promised to get a lawyer. I believed him. Six months later and still no immigration application, he came with exciting news. We would be moving from New Jersey to Virginia. I was excited to live by the ocean and away from cold winters. I believed him when he said this would be our opportunity for a fresh start. I wanted nothing more than a fresh start and I certainly didn't want to go back to Romania. I found myself giving him, once again, another chance. I found myself giving this marriage one chance after another. I found myself believing that my American dream could still come true.

As I shared previously, we didn't last a week in Virginia before Fred began his acquisitions and the fighting ensued. This was truly it for me. There would be no more chances for this marriage or that man being in our lives. I knew one person in Virginia, Macy, Fred's older brother. I met Macy after we got married at our Memorial Day marriage celebration family barbeque. Macy was the only family we had in Virginia and Hampton was our new home. Little did I know that we would only call that home for one month.

What I have learned over the years is that as long as you make a powerful decision and stay clear, committed, and determined, a way *will* be made. We don't have to know how, we just have to be willing to take the chance, and step forward into the unknown. What I understand about making a powerful decision and declaration is that it is our willingness that paves the path. Our commitment to a destination reveals the next right steps to take and the right people and opportunities show up in alignment with that decision to help us along the way. When you are willing to take the chance, the situation takes care of itself. When you are willing to take the risk, the risk pans out and often, without having to force your hand at making it work.

I didn't always understand this lesson as clearly as I am sharing it in this book, but I have known it on a subconscious level my entire life. I knew it in my bones, and it is this deep internal knowing that has caused me to take risks that have saved me and catapulted me into realms of success I only could have dreamt of before. This understanding got me out of Romania. It saved me from my abusive marriage. It has led me to careers. It has worked magic in my life.

This intuition and trust has moved me all the way through every challenge I've ever faced, and it will work for you, too. Being willing to take the risk grants you access to finding a solution to the problems you face. Intuition is not exclusive. We all have it and no one can give you theirs; you must uncover yours, let it come through, and master it. Being too afraid to move forward will always keep you stuck right where you are. You must learn to trust yourself, your vision, and your inner guidance system to walk boldly into the unknown. Being willing to leave my relationship with Fred meant being willing to face deportation. I was willing to risk it all and because I did, I gained everything; I got my life back. A new, prosperous life filled with dreams, options, and endless possibilities.

Despite that dark phase of life, I shared with you in the last chapter about some of the ways I am thriving now. I get to enjoy healthy, new relationships and friendships, watch my son thriving in his own life, I own a six-figure business, a book, and a podcast, have a network of change makers, and so much more. These are just some of the material things, but what I have really gained in my life is peace, joy, appreciation, power, bliss, and astonishment beyond belief!

I am constantly amazed at how wonderful life is simply because I was willing to take risks. I took the risk in coming to America. I took the risk of leaving my marriage. I took a risk applying for citizenship. I took multiple risks that I will continue to share with you throughout this book, but if you close the back cover of this book remembering anything; it's not about me, my life, my memories, stories, and examples. It's about the fact that *you* have this same opportunity to learn the same lessons, have the same breakthroughs, and reap unimaginable results.

You know the stories of people on their deathbed who find peace and are ready to go because they have had a FULL life? I was thinking of that while writing this book. I'm forty-four and already have had such an amazing, rich life, and I'm just reaching the half of it. Wow! Sure, I have new dreams, but I am simply awe-struck at how I have fulfilled so many of my past visions. I can hardly imagine what the future holds.

This life is so abundant if you are willing to believe it and go for it. Throughout this book, we will continue to go for it together. So, in this upcoming part about anger, I invite you to let your own anger surface. Let repressed memories show themselves to you and let yourself feel your feelings fully, in order to fully set yourself free from what keeps you stuck where you are at in your life. Let's start your healing.

Chapter 6
Nothing Left

I had been out of the shelter and living with my friend, Tatiana, in Minnesota for six months before I felt I had put myself in a new prison. While I was technically free, I was not able to live as freely as I desired. I was still not in the system. I didn't have identification, I didn't have visa status for Andrei and I. This made me feel many layers of disappointment or worthlessness. I felt so limited, reliant, and trapped.

I was doing everything I could with my VAWA application filled out by the shelter's attorney to attain my immigration status and I continued to run into snags, delays, or no response at all. I was obsessing over the mailbox waiting for correspondence from Homeland Security. I was just hoping they would send me something, anything. I was in limbo and it was unbearable. I found myself feeling so frustrated and hopeless at times. This had such a negative effect on my self esteem but certainly not my motivation. I could always see my dreams in my mind's eye; I just had no idea how to attain it, or how to fight the belief that I didn't deserve it.

One day, I finally worked up the courage to call an immigration lawyer and I was not going to hang up the phone until I got an appointment. It didn't matter when or what time, make it work no matter what. The office staff continued to warn me, "Ma'am, she's very busy. She's completely booked." I very plainly responded, "That is fine. I will call back" I got through and got to speak with Ms. Catherine, the woman who saved my life!

Something must have happened because it became clear to them that I wasn't going anywhere until I got an appointment with her. I had done everything I knew to do and I knew I couldn't figure this one out on my own. I was willing to ask for help.

Let's take a quick break from this fun little story to talk plainly about giving up all your damn pride and asking for help. Sometimes, I like to tell stories to teach lessons, and sometimes I just like to shout them at my clients with very little fluff. In fact, my clients don't get any fluff from me. I don't mind calling people out on their bullshit and when I hear a bunch of nonsense about why someone can't ask for help to get what they need, I stop them dead in their tracks. I have no problem stopping this story dead in its tracks to straight up tell you that if you aren't asking for and allowing help and support in your life, you are limiting your potential.

We are not meant to succeed alone. We are not meant to do things alone. We are a species that is built to gather. We survive and thrive together. Allowing your needs to be met by other people is a strength, not a weakness. Understanding that everyone has a unique skill set and allowing them to share their gifts with you takes humility, courage, and vulnerability that too many people are too proud to allow. Give it up, my friend. It doesn't serve you, period.

Anyway, back to this exhilarating story. The day before my appointment with Ms Catherine, I called my dad and told him, "I need $5,000 USD. I don't care if you need to sell my house or borrow the money, whatever it takes. I need it. I need it now. I'll pay you back the interest from my house sale but I need the money now. Your daughter needs it. Please help! This is for your daughter and your grandson!"

After my first divorce, I had my own house built. Partially to distract myself with a project and partially to prove I was fine on my own. When I moved to America, I put everything in my dad's name. Since the time I left, the house had been on the market but I didn't sell. The 2007 - 2009 recession hit Romania too. I was now calling my dad in 2010 with still no sale but that didn't stop me from asking. I would stop at nothing to get us our green cards.

Catherine took my binder, filled with copies and originals of all my documents and all the forms I had sent to the Home Land Security office for the past year. She looked over them very quickly, and let me know that they were filled out completely wrong. This made a whole lot of sense as to why I was getting nowhere with them. Are you getting the point about allowing help yet? You don't know everything there is to know about everything *and* you don't need to. Stop making life harder than it has to be and let yourself be helped.

Catherine was so interested and inspired by my determination and history that she decided to take on my case, pro bono. That means free. She took on my case for free because I was willing to take the risk of sitting with the determination of getting the help I needed. But wait, there's more. Just after she let me know she'd be taking my case, she brought in an immigration divorce attorney who also took on my case pro bono. After more than a year of struggling with paperwork that I did not understand for a process that I did not know, in one day's time two people were placed in my life that would grant me liberation from so many of my troubles and give me the chance I needed for that fresh start I was praying for.

I was so frustrated and angry with my situation that I decided I would do anything and everything in my power to change it; including show-ing others how committed I am to the process, and people saw it. They saw me and they were willing to help me. The same way Macy saw me, the shelter volunteer employees, and my childhood friend, Tatiana, from Romania, Catherine came through for me to help, guide, and advise. She saved me. She saved us.

"Okay, find yourself a place to live and start looking for a job. First thing we will do is apply for your authorization for work, so you can pay your rent and provide for your family. Go find yourself a job," she immediately advised me.

"But...but I don't have any documentation," I stammered, scared shitless of what she just told me to do.

"I know, and you will very soon. We will get you your authorization to work. That's my job, don't worry about it. Let me do my job. You go do yours. Find work "

I had no idea how to do what she was asking of me but if she was willing to believe in her own skills, I would, too. I didn't know what I was doing but I was willing to take the risk.

I was so nervous as I applied for jobs without documentation. I had no papers. No visa. No ID. Nothing. I was not in the system but I was apply-ing like I was. I was applying purely on faith, grit, resilience, and deter-mination to make this work and to set myself free.

After applying for job after job, I finally got a call back for an interview. I don't remember the content of that phone interview but I do remember how happy I was when she said "Come in for an in-person interview." Just a few hours before that first interview, I got the call from Catherine that my card had come in and she asked me to come down to her office to pick it up. Again, this was just a few hours before my interview. This was all happening on the same day - and now I had to make it to Ms. Catherine's office first. It took me well up to an hour to get anywhere those days because I had to take the bus.

That bus ride in rainy cold, grey, fall in Minnesota was like a dream. I saw all my past two years flashing in front of my eyes; all the confusion, fights, yelling, hopelessness and despair. Here I am, in two years' time having moved from Romania to Jersey to Virginia to Minnesota and about to get a piece of my new identity, a work visa for the US. I am a person, in the system. Still with an alien number - but in the system. I can work now, legally! I was so excited that I forgot about all the nerves for the upcoming job interview. The concept of "possibilities" was being redefined for me.

While it was a very pleasant surprise, the fact that I got my work authorization card one hour before the first job interview I had landed seemed like no mistake to me. The timing of it all amazed me. It was too obvious to ignore. Coincidence? No! I don't believe in those anymore. I was constantly solidifying my faith in courageously taking the steps into the unknown. Risk-taking one could say, for me feels more like stretching myself from what is familiar and safe. I was learning that raising your voice isn't about volume, it's about sheer determination. You don't have to shout to raise your voice: you have to say what you mean and mean what you say. Specificity and clarity are way more powerful and effective than volume.

Taking a stand for what you believe in and believing it right into existence is about the decision to have what you desire and go for it fully. There is really no space for fear. You might be scared like I was when I was applying for jobs but I did it anyway. Getting what you want is about committing to what you want and moving beyond fear to go get it.

No authorization, no job, no money, no opportunity was going to come knocking on my door. I had to go out and get it, and so I did. Everyone, including you, has this option available to you. If a Romanian immigrant with very little English skills and connections can acquire a job, so can you. If that same immigrant can become a global citizen, make six figures, and redefine the construct of family, you can move past your fears and barriers to attain anything you could possibly want.

Speaking of what I wanted, I let Catherine know I needed to leave her office quickly because it would take me another hour to get to that interview.

"You're a ten minute car ride away from that location. I will take you. Let's just talk about this interview..." She coached me a little bit and gave me some interview tips. I felt as ready as I could but that didn't make me feel any less nervous. I wanted this job more than anything I could remember wanting. Getting a job meant staying in America. I knew nothing would stop me from achieving my dreams.

Catherine dropped me in front of the building and with a warm smile and confident voice she said, "You are getting this job. This job is yours."

Upon my arrival, the manager was too busy to even see me. When I walked in, there were people everywhere. It was chaotic and nerve-wracking. I remember the clicking of my heels but all I could hear was the hum of people talking, hustling, and bustling.

When I walked up to the desk, I did not realize that I was talking directly to the owner that would be interviewing me. I was so nervous. I was still pretty self-conscious about my English skills and she seemed preoccupied by how busy the store was. When I walked up and asked to speak with Tammie, she looked at me with wide eyes and admitted that she forgot she had an interview. She hurriedly told me to wait in the break room.

When I went to the break room, my heart was racing. I was trying to catch my breath and I sat there for just a minute before noticing how messy it was back there. I started cleaning and organizing in my head and within minutes, I grabbed a broom and started sweeping. It helped me catch my breath and calm my nerves.

I really caught my breath and some rhythm because I just continued sweeping into the store. With my hands on the broom and my head down, I nearly forgot where I was. Doing something familiar had me feeling in my element and it must have shown. When Tammie saw me sweeping between clients, she immediately stopped, turned, pointed at me and said, "You're hired!" and went back to what she was doing. Without a single moment of an interview, I now had a job.

A huge wave of relief swept over me and I felt my shoulders drop. I simply kept sweeping for the time being, only now with a smile on my face and some pep in my step. I was now sweeping at my place of work. I went from feeling like an outsider, constantly trying to earn her keep, to an employee with a place to call work.

I wandered around the store sort of in slow motion wondering, "What just happened? Is this a joke?" When the customers left one by one and the store was empty, we finally sat down and talked. Except it wasn't really an interview, just the logistics of my new job. I tried to play it cool when I just wanted to do a happy dance, but Tammie just spoke so matter of factly that I became focused. She explained, "we will start a two week trial, I will train and teach you, we will start with a part-time job position. Here are the days, the hours, and your hourly rate." She was writing and talking so quickly that it was difficult for me to keep up with her; I was so excited and overwhelmed.

It never ceases to amaze me that I had gotten a job that I applied for without authorization to work simply because I was willing to pick up a broom and do what I knew to do. It had worked. My faith had worked. My commitment had worked. My belief in myself was finally working out.

It has always been my willingness to try that has gotten me through the trying times. Even if I struggled with my belief, I have always been encouraged to keep trying and I was always willing to believe that things could get better. A lot of my circumstances would seem to be proving the opposite but I was always willing to hold onto my vision for a better future.

How does your vision, or lack thereof, cause or prevent your future? Are you willing to take that step out of your comfort zone? Are you willing to give it your all? Are you willing to show up determined day after day *after day* to show others, yourself, and a higher power that you are committed to a better future? Are you willing to commit to your dream as if that is it, with no backup plan? I invite you to look in the areas of your life in which you quit too soon, give up too easily, and shy away from opportunity just because you aren't willing to stretch outside of your comfort zone.

There is technically no reason I should have gotten that interview and yet, I applied with conviction. I got the interview. I got my authorization for work. I even got a ride to my interview. I don't know how it all worked out. I just know that when you're willing to go for it, the *how* works itself out.

This is not new information to anyone with faith and commitment. When you are willing to believe in your dream, the path is made. When you are unwilling to believe, the path becomes overgrown and unclear and you become consumed by doubt and struggle. You must be willing to give up your doubt, fear, and insecurity to be able to have the courage to step far beyond what logic and reason says. When chasing big, audacious dreams, predictably, the right thing to do is to take steps far beyond logic and reason. You must be willing to take that step.

Taking all of these steps myself led me to working a job that I loved with a boss that I loved and afforded me my new apartment. It also led me to my third husband. Dean was the IVF Laboratory Director at the Mayo Clinic, with half of the alphabet after his name, and his work was world renowned.

We met at my work on my birthday. It might sound cliche, but yes, I believe he was a gift for me, just didn't know at the time what kind of gift. It was a big day for me. Not because it was my birthday, but because I was moving that day, and I couldn't wait to get home and move. We were moving to the best place we had ever lived in that town. It was our fourth address in the past three years in that town alone. It was a three bed-room townhome, in a neighborhood with young families with kids whom Andrei could play with. We got to have a porch, a large, shared backyard and heated pool. Andrei got to be outside and play with children! I was *so* excited! It was a dream come true.

That day, I was wearing jeans, so not the way I would normally dress at work, and a blue shirt with a giant "24" on it, my day of birth. Cheesy, I know, but I was celebrating! Dean walks in looking for eyewear and like I would do with any other customer, I invite him to sit down in front of the mirror and bring him some options and offer him a full consultation on the what, how, and why for each frame.

Dean was nothing like I would ever go for in a man but he was appealing and couldn't figure out why I was attracted to him. He was charming in a way that I had never noticed before. Because I was growing, changing, and evolving, I believe my taste in men changed as well. Never before would I go after a guy like Dean but there was just something about him.

He was appealing to me in a brand new way. It started with him stopping by for "an adjustment" until I called him out on his BS, "Your frames are perfect, no adjustment needed. If you want to stop by to see me, that's okay, but leave the frames alone." He blushed like a kid and I was moved by his reaction. He must have not known what he was getting into with a European woman because we don't play cutsie games, we cut straight to the chase.

Something else that was new to me was that Dean truly made it safe to trust him. He made it safe to love and made me feel safe in intimacy. Based on my previous relationships, this was the most valuable thing a man could offer me in a relationship. Sex, great. Career, great. Travel, great. Life, great. Trust, intimacy, and safety? Hook, line, and sinker.

At this point in my life, these aspects of my relationship were so important. I still had my own work to do in recovering from traumas of my past marriages and yet, we grew together and supported each other's growth so much. It was very clear to both of us that we entered each other's lives for very important reasons. We grew our relationship and I also grew my relationship with myself.

I was making my own money and taking care of myself. Just before I had met Dean, I truly realized that I did not need a man to sustain my life or become successful. Because of this, our relationship had a different dynamic to it. We chose to be with each other. We didn't *need* each other. We got to enjoy each other in a whole new way and I got to enjoy life in a whole new way.

Because I was enjoying life in a whole new way, I started to notice my distaste for Minnesota, snow, and winter. I was sharing with Dean that I wanted to live in constant summer, near the water, on the beach, somewhere beautiful. While our dating was going great, I was ready to move and I wanted to relocate before Andrei started high school. Remember when we talked earlier about the clarity of what we want and letting go of how it will happen? Well, I kid you not, two weeks after that conversation, Dean asked me, "How far are you willing to move?" He had just gotten a job offer in New Zealand.

Dean took me with him to different fertility conferences around the world. At the same time, I started a new career and traveled to my own conferences in the coaching world and he would join me too. Before we knew it, we were this traveling couple from New Zealand. "He would be traveling in Malaysia, she would be traveling to Texas, and they'd meet up in Spain." It felt like a real-life fairy tale playing out. In my work, I focused on supporting the LGBTQ community and wanted to learn about alternative fertility options for those seeking it. Having had the opportunity to learn firsthand from the scientists and experts in the field was such a blessing and a privilege.

Traveling alongside Dean and attending conferences in the fertility world opened up doors in the field for me, as well. I had a badge behind the scenes and backstage. It gave me the opportunity to speak to people I may have never otherwise had access to. Similar to my relationship with my freedoms and liberties in becoming an American citizen, I knew the caliber of the opportunity right in front of me and I was completely honored by the blessing. It was something that I always respected and that I never took for granted. I have thoroughly enjoyed every magical situation I have found myself in.

While this was wonderful, exciting, and fun, I'll never forget the most special moment of all. During a cocktail hour, I was socializing and bouncing from one conversation to another. There were so many times that Dean would end up deep in a conversation and I would end up on the other side of the room, chatting it up with someone else. One night, I remember looking over and seeing Dean smiling at me and staring at me as though he had a crush on me. In a fun, refreshing way, it felt like we were strangers falling in love all over again.

I remember him acknowledging me later that night when it was just the two of us. He shared how grateful he was that I could hold my own at these events. I could hold a conversation, make a connection, and even leave a positive impression with total strangers in his crowd. We would even joke how I didn't know what a stranger was because I could make anyone my friend. He loved this about me and I loved being his wife. I had never felt appreciated in this way before and his opinion, admiration, and respect for me were very important to me. I wanted to make him proud. I loved us at the events together and I enjoyed the parties where we got to take over the dance floor and just have fun, as though the whole event was for us.

I started my *Redefined Family in the Modern Age of LGBTQ* Podcast and also extended my coaching in this arena. This put me in the fertility and LGBTQ space, which allowed me to interview leaders of the world on my podcast, for people to hear directly from some of the biggest names in the industry. This was such a fun time in the growth and development of my business. This phase led to endless opportunities, and continues to.

I have been to conferences and seminars across the globe. I have spoken on the TEDx stage as my first talk ever, the Health Coach Institute as a "$10K in 10 Weeks Challenge" finalist, and won. I also spoke at the International Surrogacy Conference in line with fertility experts, speakers my husband included, radio shows, podcasts, pride events and many more. Dean supported my new career and growth consistently and cheered me on from the first row, sharing his admiration of my commitment and discipline. He has truly believed in me and in what I'm capable of.

From feeling like I have nothing left sitting in Catherine's office to feeling like I have everything at my fingertips, I remind myself every day to go for all of it! Never back down, never quit, never talk myself out of anything. It doesn't matter how bleak or dire a situation might seem, there is endless possibility on the other side of stepping beyond anger, fear, frustration, and resentment. You can have it all if you're willing to go for it.

So, when you feel like you have nothing left, go within and find one shred of faith, energy, and power and take it with you on your way towards your fullest life. Take one step in that direction. Just that one step. All you have to do now is take that step in front of you to keep moving toward your dreams. You can do it. Step forward.

Chapter 7

Raising My Voice

Becoming a woman who could speak up in an intimidating environment is no accident. Being able to hold a conversation with complete strangers and leave an event with friends is regular to me. Walking in somewhere as a nobody and leaving with everybody knowing my name is second nature to me. I love living out loud nowadays but that certainly wasn't always the case.

I wish I knew what all of my trials and tribulations would accumulate to when I was a little girl. Shit, even as a thirty-three year old woman, I wish I knew that what I was going through would make sense one day - but that's besides the point. As a thirteen-year-old and the youngest of three, I struggled with so much stress and anxiety. When I moved from the country to the city to live with my Aunt to be able to attend a better school in the city, I felt lost, alone, and *really* stupid.

Making the transition in middle school was such an awful experience because on my first day of my new school, I had the realization that I didn't know anything. School in the country was much more simple and far behind than school in the city. I struggled with so much internal dialog about being an idiot, dumb, and so far behind. Embarrassment seemed to be a permanent feeling within me. This was a time when bullying was allowed. I was called names by both my teacher and my peers. I was reminded daily about how uneducated I was, just a country girl, with no proper manners, or proper speech. Judging others was something that everyone would do and I was the perfect target. I was judged daily.

I remember crying to my teachers, begging them to tutor me, mentor me, to catch me up with my peers. I knew that I couldn't catch up on my own and getting help was my only hope to get into a good high school. It was humiliating when one teacher said, "there is no way in hell you're going to *that* high school."

At first, this scared me, because I believed them. Although I felt so low, I knew that I could not, and would not, let this happen. This is really when I began to find my voice, my inner spark. It was the conception of the 'me' that I am today. At this phase of my life, it didn't show up by speaking up or making demands. It showed up in my actions. I set my sights on getting into the best high school and got to work on my studies. My middle name might as well have been "Determined" because I had decided that no teacher's opinion of me was going to keep me out of high school. I became hellbent on proving everyone, including myself, wrong about being behind, stupid, or unworthy of getting a great education.

These were some of the most stressful times of my young life because I would sleep two hours a night. I would basically nap just enough to get back up, study, go to school, work, and study more. I taught myself what I needed to. I worked as hard as I could to memorize, understand, and comprehend all of these concepts that were so much more advanced than what I had been taught in the country. I remember my aunt calling my parents worried about me not sleeping enough and studying at night. When I got a low grade, it was hell. I would do nothing but study. I was not hungry, I was not tired, all I wanted was to learn to correct that grade.

My studies went on like this for the rest of that school year. The next year, my last year of middle school, my teachers saw the growth in me. I was starting to catch up academically and everyone around me was noticing. I knew I was making real progress when I finally earned math tutoring. In Romania, you have to earn what you get. I earned tutoring not because anyone had sympathy for me or wanted to help me catch up. I had to prove I was worth helping for anyone to decide to spend their time with me.

I was so proud of myself, but never stopped working hard. Once I made it to the point of earning people's approval, I started working harder just to keep it and not lose it. This was a different kind of stress, especially when I had earned the option to choose my high school. I had three options in the city and chose the one that afforded me the opportunity to study math and physics at the top high school.

Any bit of excitement for earning a top spot in my high school selection process was stomped out when I let my parents know which school I had picked and my dad told me not to come home. The high school that I chose was his *third* option and he was furious with me. It was not an option at all. I was supposed to become a teacher or a doctor. "Choosing a math and physics high school will prepare you for what? Not for a real job!" he said harshly. It didn't matter what I wanted, what I had become good at, or what I was being recognized for, he wanted his way and he wanted me to choose what he wanted.

This crushed me. I had slaved away on my education to come up from behind and I was exiled for it. On graduation day of middle school, I got a prize as second in my class and the principal praised me in front of everyone about my huge progress in such a short time. It was nice, but it didn't matter; my parents weren't there. They were off working the land in the country. That was more important to them. I had never felt so lonely, unnoticed, or unappreciated, like I didn't matter.

It was so frustrating to have gone through all that work to make a name for myself and still feel rejected by my father. It took some time to make peace with that. I was still very young and like most children, I wanted my parents' approval. What I realized in that situation was that I was going to have to make my choices. I felt very alone during that time but it caused me to rely on myself, which we all know would become very valuable later in life.

I did not change my selection. I did not back down nor did I apologize for it. I stood my ground, and affirmed that I wanted to study math and physics where I had the best opportunity to do so. I raised my voice. I spoke up. I stood up for what I wanted and I went for it and at the same, time I felt rebellious. I felt disrespectful for not obeying, because where I come from, that's what raising your voice meant.

I had already pushed myself to the edge of my comfort zone, stressing myself out over teaching myself to catch up and keep up. I wasn't about to let my dad's opinion of my future change it. As a fourteen-year-old, just because I was determined to be independent didn't mean that this situation didn't hurt. I was scared, but determined. Both *can* coexist.

This changed the dynamic of my relationship with my parents. I did my best to come to terms with the fact that they weren't accepting of me or my choices. It felt as though if I wasn't obeying or letting them control me, then I wasn't their daughter. I decided that if that is what being a daughter meant, I would find a way to make it on my own, and so I did.

From there, I had a very rigorous schooling experience. I studied and did everything I could to be at the top of my class. This paid off and taught me so much, and as I have shared, led to a very bright future of being brave enough to go for big dreams and not settle for what others told me that I should be doing. Even at that age, I was earning more money than most of my peers and I was successful, competitive, and passionate. I learned to raise my voice very young and it has served me greatly throughout my life. I only wish that fourteen-year-old could have realized exactly what she was working for. Maybe then, she could have experienced a bit of relief from the pain and anxiety.

By the time I was forty, I was attending dozens of events, some with Dean, some by myself, all around the world. They were packed with world leaders and I knew what it meant to stand on my own. I was more than excited to raise my voice and raise my hand when it came to opportunities to collaborate, coordinate, and interview leaders of this world. It was incredible to share their missions and voices on my *Redefined Family in the Modern Age of LGBTQ* Podcast.

The skills I built as a young girl allowed me to raise my voice when it was time to speak on the TedX stage and share my message of unconditional love, acceptance, and breaking all stereotypes. It has allowed me to raise my voice against discrimination and labels.

Speaking up for myself as a thirteen-year-old also taught me how to speak up against people doubting and judging me in Romania after my first divorce. It helped me speak up against Fred and get out of my abusive marriage. It helped me get that first job, my visa, my career, and the list goes on and on. Raising my voice has raised my vibration as well as the quality of my life, since the moment I learned how to do it. Everything that we do, all the steps we take, are contributing to what we create. That being said, it is important to give our best at all times, because it turns out that our effort is worth it. We can always get more than we wish from life if we are open to receiving. Everything compounds and grows exponentially. It always comes back to us bigger and richer than we could have anticipated. If you are willing to believe this and remain open to possibility, you will see it manifest in your reality.

Because this book is for you as much as it is for me, it is important to take this opportunity to look at the pivotal points of your life that have shaped who you have become. What happened in your life that didn't make sense back then and has become an integral part of your success now?

Another area to look at is where you stay quiet in your life. Here are a few journaling prompts to get serious about if you are serious about being a bold leader and achieving greatness:

- Where do you let others speak for you and make your decisions?
- Where do you silence yourself and your desires?
- What stops you from speaking up about what you see and want?
- What do you want?

That 'what do you want' question can be an interesting one. For me, it is the most powerful question! I built my whole business around this question. I am always building, redefining, and refining my life around the answers to this question. This is the question that I ask myself and my clients the most. It never gets old because the answer is always new as we grow and evolve.

So much of what we have learned to want comes from our upbringing. If I agreed to what my dad wanted, I really don't want to imagine the direction my life would have gone in. So when journaling about what you want, consider what you have been conditioned to want and become a bit more critical about where your desires originated. Pay attention to *who* is answering this question. Is it the answer yours or someone else's?

This will help you shed any small Self beliefs and desires that stop you from becoming your most authentic self. Starting with what you want might be confusing or distracting. When you take a closer look at who you *really* are and be honest about what's important to *you*, what you want will more or less reveal itself to you. This is not easy. It takes courage and vulnerability to be honest and voice our hearts' desires.

For example, when I realized that I really care about everyone better understanding unconditional love, I wanted to become a public speaker. This wasn't always a dream of mine. Being an author wasn't a goal before I knew I had a story to tell. It was only by meeting more of myself that I discovered what that self wanted for herself.

Coach Simona, here to instruct! Once you take the time to make your list of desires, I invite you to read it out loud in the mirror, looking right into your own eyes. In a later chapter, I will share the absolute magic of writing down your dreams. For now, I want to make it known that it is time to start speaking what you want out loud. Remember, silence kills. It murders possibility and the process of manifesting your desires. Your spoken word has power. Although invisible coming out of your mouth, words are physical objects. Speak as if your words build your life, because they do. Speak as if you say book, a book will fall out of your mouth. If you say money, it will fill your bank account. If you speak hurt and harm, you will create that too.

My friend, it is time to get much more serious about the words coming out of your mouth. Hire new words that can build your dream and fire the ones that can destroy it. It is time to raise your voice. It is time to raise your vibration. It is time to raise the quality of your life. Onward and upward.

Chapter 8

A Whole New Level of Being Lost

This chapter is subtly one of the most near and dear to my heart. It is titled 'a whole new level of being lost' because almost every time I thought I had made it to the end of a spiral full of struggle, I seemed to enter a new one. I used to have a victim mentality about this process but then, I recognized it as just that: a process. I think so many people trip from one spiral into another without ever recognizing the lessons these spirals are meant to offer.

I love to use the spiral as a metaphor in my talks and coaching. I will use this reference throughout the rest of this book and I think that, upwards or downwards, a spiraling feeling depicts the learning process we go through in the different phases of our lives. If we play close attention, we may notice that we are going through the same experience over and over again until we complete a circle. The way we respond to it takes us up a level or we stagnate, looping in that circle until we learn the lesson. So, we come to the same point again until we learn what we need to in order to grow and to evolve.

The same goes with pain. It's not that it doesn't hurt next time, it's just that we know how to manage it faster and with less blame, resentment, and anger. During the next spiral, we learn how to go through the pain, heal, and release all negativity from it. Each spiral takes us higher in life but as you can tell, life goes on. There is always the possibility of pain, failure, disappointment, or loss. The difference is that when you evolve through each lesson spiral, you become a more evolved person who can handle more.

For the sake of your sanity and the quality of your life, it is important to find the lessons in everything and turn obstacles into opportunities. When we see the lessons for what they are trying to teach, we naturally uplevel in life and find ourselves operating at a new baseline. When we go upward on the spiral, this can become quite magical. I have seen unimaginable results manifest in my own life.

The process of gaining residency in another country is more than just a paperwork process. An immigrant often faces discrimination, rejection, and outright refusal when trying to gain access to their rights on forgein land. As I shared early on, teaching people the immigration experience is a passion of mine because it is so easy to judge what we don't know or don't understand. It is even easier to turn a blind eye and deaf ear to this portion of the population because we are often seen as intrusive or inva-sive. There is a "you wouldn't have these problems if you would just go back to your own country" flavor of rejection that makes it hard to speak up about what we go up against in our journey.

When I referenced anger and breaking points at the start of this sec-tion, I started with the immigration process in mind. In fact, whether it was in my marriage, career, health, wealth, or something else, every single aspect of my life has been impacted by the immigration process. It impacted my identity, who I am, how I behave, and how I see the world. This conversation has ruled my life for a solid decade. My quality of life was dictated by my status, which was determined by other individuals' decisions. So much of my personal and professional timeline has also been shaped by the deadlines and timelines of the immigration process, and if you don't like going to the DMV for your license, imagine going for it every year after year, for four years. Having one-year-valid documentation is like living with this one year expiration date hanging on your neck. It's tiresome and defeating. The anger that this process has surfaced in me has brought up some of my most unflattering, unrefined moments. As the subject of discrimination, I've learned about the topic in a brand new way.

I have felt pretty out of place for most of my life, but the journey of getting my US citizenship involved a whole new level of feeling lost. When I was rejected by my family or friends in Romania, I felt like I had a different foundation to stand on. Maybe it was being in my home country or feeling like I could take care of myself, but in America, I felt helpless so much of the time. I felt constantly discriminated against, judged, and shunned. I will never forget the rage I experienced at the DMV office when the woman behind the desk took my different colored form, looked at me with a snotty face and an eye roll, and said "Oh, you're one of *those*."

It took everything within me not to reach across her desk, punch her in the face, and take some of her hair out. I had done everything I could to be an upstanding, contributing member of society. I was a law-abiding citizen with no right to vote. I paid the same rent, same bills, went to work, paid my taxes, after-school programs, and summer daycare. I did all the same things, like any American, but because my authorization had a one year expiration date, everything else was only valid for one year as well: my work contract, my driver's license, my insurance, everything! So, therefore everything I had, I had to renew every year! Are you tired of reading 'every year' yet? Imagine living on such annual terms in every single aspect of your life. It was utterly exhausting.

I could have stopped at just maintaining my residency, but becoming an American citizen and fully integrating into the culture included being an educated voter, and that was important to me. Because I didn't stop, I faced years of more obstacles and those 'lesson spirals' I mentioned earlier; I may call them loops from time to time if I am feeling fancy. What wasn't obvious to me at the time was I was just relearning important life lessons at a whole new level.

I didn't exactly realize it, but I was using the same skills I learned in my adolescence when I chose a high school and my dad said "Don't come home." In this case, I had chosen America, and complete strangers were trying to make me feel like it wasn't my home. It was such a demoralizing experience to try to prove your worth to people who aren't interested in granting you any. It felt like a constant fight, a constant battle, and it certainly activated plenty of anger within me. It activated the thirteen-year-old who felt rejected, but I did what I had learned to do; I raised my voice. I started shifting from being a victim to each situation or circumstance, and instead observed when it was time to raise my voice, take a stand, or look for a new approach. This made a world of difference in my immigration process. I was no longer tripping from loop to loop unconsciously.

The more aware and intentional I became, I watched judgment, discrimination, and disregard come in so many forms; some were direct, some discrete. Most of the time, I understood it was because of American ignorance about immigrants and immigration. So many Americans do not truly understand what we face and have a generalized story about the majority of us. One may dehumanize and clump us together to justify their view of immigrants, but they miss out on meeting each of us for how unique we are. Americans who immediately reject immigrants don't know the environments we've come from and don't know what we've gone through to get where we are. This puts everyone at the disadvantage of separation and disconnection. Looking from the other direction is a valid point, as well. Immigrants can't expect Americans to adapt to their culture and way of living. As we choose (most of us) to come to this country, we are the ones to adapt and calibrate into this culture. It takes commitment from both parties to make the conscious effort of understanding and accepting each other.

I feel strongly about uniting people of the world from all ages, races, religions, cultures, genders, orientations, vocations, and any other differences because of the basic rule of interdependence: we are better together. As a species, we were created to rely on each other. There will never be one person, or one type of person, that is the one-size-fits-all solution to humanity. It is our immense variety that keeps us thriving. Learning to not only accept, but also celebrate each other is essential to overcoming humanity's greatest obstacles.

I share about American ignorance because I have seen it firsthand. I wish it was only my experience, but unfortunately, it is how many immigrants feel. I use the term 'ignorance' because it means inexperience or lack of awareness. It is not an insult, rather an observation of how little American citizens interact with immigrants. I'll never forget the day I got my US citizenship. My family were all in Romania and my husband and son had already moved to New Zealand. So, on the day I swore in as a US citizen, I was surrounded by a handful of friends in Minnesota. I was hosted by one of my former clients, Anne, who invited a few friends and threw me a surprise party. It was a party full of fifty and sixty-plus-year-old, white Midwesterners, and at one point, one of them asked me why I came to the US.

When I told them a bit of my history, I turned that party into a funeral. I shared my upbringing. I talked about Communist Romania. I shared truthfully about my immigration journey, my abusive marriage, plus some of my most fearful times and my darkest hours as a single mom with a young child. People were stunned.

Even though the party went on like normal, one person came up to me and personally apologized to me. I was a bit confused by this because I did not feel offended by him but he explained that had never truly taken the time to really meet an immigrant and understand their story and history. Clearly apologizing straight from the heart, he said that me sharing my experience had changed his perspective completely.

I appreciated this so much. It brought me a sense of peace that I hadn't felt in a while. While this didn't erase the past, it made up for a few memories of being discriminated against. It was so phenomenal and it was really the first time that I understood that it is not always true that Americans don't accept us, it is that they don't understand us. It reminded me that so many people act the way they do because they are clueless and don't take the time to learn. Worse off, they never end up in a situation with the opportunity to learn. Americans can be so sheltered and uninformed that they never get firsthand exposure. This is detrimental to our connection, understanding, and acceptance of one another.

A major reason why I committed to writing this book was to share and show that our stories are not fake. What we deal with is real, and it's hell. Coming to the US is a dream for millions around the world and yet, so many Americans take it for granted. I do not say or share this to shame Americans. If I can make a difference in this world, it would be to open up the eyes, ears, minds, and hearts of every person so that we may coexist harmoniously. Everyone, not just Americans. It may be a lifetime project, and I am up for the task.

I had a whole new task on my hands shortly after moving to New Zealand with Dean in 2016. I definitely found myself surprised about how lost I felt when we moved there. I thought moving to the island would be a total vacation lifestyle filled with fun, sun, sand, and success. I had spent all of those years in America working hard to get my documentation and be an approved citizen only to move to New Zealand and feel like I entered yet another new prison, but at least a prettier one. I had tripped straight from one spiral into another without recognizing what happened. This was much more of an emotional prison than a captive, abusive, or discriminatory situation.

New Zealand has a very interesting culture. The first barrier, believe it or not, was the language. As an English as a second language speaker who was doing pretty well for where she was, I felt like I had to learn English all over again. To this day, I still have a hard time understanding the kiwi accent. Then, I ran into a very 'locals only' type of island mentality that gives tourists, namely me, a feeling of resistance. I felt this resistance very strongly and it surfaced some of the insecurities that I was able to ignore and work out in America. I felt rejected and unaccepted in new ways. While applying for my citizenship in the US, I could still fill out those different colored forms and things would work out for me. I didn't let it matter how mean or nasty people were to me, if they misunderstood me, or judged me. I just kept turning in my paperwork. On the island, it was a new type of rejection.

I think that Americans may judge and discriminate to make foreigners feel unwelcome for fear of them invading their land and taking their jobs or husbands, but the locals of New Zealand seemed to have a much deeper disdain for *any* non-natives. After all, with my Romanian accent, I wasn't exactly pegged as an American; I just wasn't a New Zealander. While many people have no resistance integrating there, that was not my experience.

This was pretty disappointing at first but instead of getting too caught up in this feeling, I decided to shift my focus heavily toward going back to school to start my business and get my coaching certification. I studied, developed, and grew a business to six-figures. I may have not been able to connect with New Zealand culture or its people but I was able to connect with myself, my clarity, passion, and vision, and go for it fully. I stopped trying to make friends and build networks on the island and got creative. I redirected my focus to the online space.

This time of isolation on the island kept me home to study, work, and create, and that's exactly what I did. So, while I loved the island, weather, water, and my home there, I didn't spend too much time trying to integrate myself into any communities anymore. I attained real estate in the online world and established my new residency in virtual communities and networks. Making this shift helped me take my focus off of feeling trapped on an island in the middle of the ocean to having the world at my fingertips, and that move has set me free for the rest of my life. Remember when I said that all the steps we take matter? This particular step served me very well four years later when the world-wide pandemic hit. While people struggled with working from home and moving their work online, I was already there.

During the four years of living in New Zealand, I traveled the most I have in my life. While it was so exotic to say "I'm living in New Zealand" or greeting my people online with, "Hello from the future," I couldn't cover up that I didn't want to be there. Two things became very obvious to me. One, I was always excited to be off the island and took every chance I could. Second, traveling from so far became hard on my health and well-being. New Zealand remains my favorite place in the world, the Paradise on Earth. I realized that it was a place I wanted to visit, but living there was not for me.

As my business continued to grow and I began to feel more successful, I knew that I was now at a crossroads. I could maintain my New Zealand residency and continue to compromise my desire for a lifestyle of traveling and in-person connection, networking, and building a physical community around me, or I could choose to make a big, bold move back across the ocean to a place that I love, excites me, and better suits me. I decided that I was going to be moving back to America, specifically to Los Angeles. The plan was to make this move when Andrei graduated high school. Little did I know, this would happen much earlier.

I love LA. I love being near the water. I love the year round summer, sunshine, and I *love* the people. So many people in Los Angeles thrive on the same focus, energy, passion, and entrepreneurial spirit that I do. My soul always recognizes when I am wandering around Southern California and I am filled with inspiration and excitement. Beyond the city limits of LA, having an international airport and direct flights to pretty much everywhere in the world gives me the freedom I crave and love.

I knew that I was ready to create a shift in my life and so I decided to go for it. Spending four years generally isolated on an island prepared me to stand on my own two feet in a new way. I may have tripped into that emotional spiral but I made it out on the other side, clearer and stronger. You will begin to notice the upleveling as I continue to share my story, and you will be able to notice it in your life, too.

As I mentioned in the beginning of this chapter, an interesting lesson that I have only learned through understanding the various 'spiral' experiences of life, is that we are always learning the same lesson over and over while climbing higher and higher. When I thought I was alone in Romania was different than when I thought I was alone in America, which was different than when I thought I was alone in New Zealand. I felt alone at each stage, but in new ways, and I knew it was because I was different at each level. I was stronger and wiser with each new loop on the spiral. I was upleveling my experience.

I have always pushed the limits and raised the ceiling of success, but what was subtly happening at the same time was that I was raising my baseline. The entire time, I was raising and strengthening the foundation of my life. By the time I was ready to leave New Zealand, I was standing on my own foundation, a foundation that I knew I had laid on my own.

The magic of this is the elevation of each experience. To shift from a baseline of isolation of mental and emotional abuse to the isolation of living on an island where it was hard to make connections are vastly different baselines. Both were lonely and both are relative. I think that this is so important to understand because we tend to ignore the problems of the fortunate because they may not be visibly struggling.

I saw clear evidence of this in the work I have done in the LGBTQ communities and families I have worked with. On the outside, these people may have jobs, cars, homes, food, and fortune, but they are struggling silently with the rejection of their parents. They may be suffering over discrimination or loss that comes with their sexual orientation. They may be struggling with their own identity and feel a whole new level of being lost than struggling for food, safety, and shelter. Unfortunately, higher baseline struggles get diminished with terms like "First World problems" and get ignored. This can be detrimental to the population's welfare because most people's most serious problems are invisible and many stay silent about them because they don't feel safe to speak up.

If we decide whose struggles are worse, we are simply judging. This denies people the help, resources, and support they need to heal and thrive. I was in a dire situation when I left Virginia. Everyone could see and agree that I needed help. When I was married, building a business, and living on an island, people might not have taken my struggles as seriously, but I did. I have explained the upleveling up my lifestyle but parallel to it was upleveling my relationships over time. This raised my baseline for the types of men I allow in my life and heart.

This evolution was so obvious to me in my marriage with Dean. Dean was patient with me in so many ways. It is often said that you end up in relationships with people that "match your vibe." I wasn't brought up talking about manifestation and frequency, so I still laugh about all the terms people use for making shit happen. But, because there is no Romanian translation for vibe, I will use the woo-woo words. Dean and I were a perfect match for each other when we got together. I could easily see how we were meant to be together as we supported each other through our next phases of respective growth.

I have had so much trauma from my childhood and past relationships that trust, love, and affection have been very difficult for me. Dean was patient, kind, gentle, and understanding as I practiced vulnerability, connection, and healthy communication. We didn't always get it right but we were at least willing to practice with each other. He was my 'home.' He was my safe space to share authentically and unapologetically. Not only was he my first cheerleader, he was also ready to hear me with a nonjudgmental ear and hold me with his loving, caring, and big arms.

I also saw my role in his life. Being an established scientist and leader, Dean is a geek who is business and detail-oriented. This comes with a type of facade that can be a challenge in a relationship with others, and even with himself. I got to help him with communication, connection, reciprocation, and love in my own ways, too. Our relationship stretched us both to keep sharing our love with one another without wanting to run and hide. It was a challenge we were both committed to but we kept showing up for the challenge. I helped him in his relationship with himself, his career, and definitely with his fashion sense!

Over the years, our relationship has had its ups and downs, and yet, I am always and forever grateful for what we have been able to do for each other. The places we have gone and the way that life has guided us through our journey side-by-side is something I will never take for granted. I have been lost at many points in my life. The path of life has spun me around and has made me dizzy in the darkness of those spirals, loops, and circles, but life with Dean definitely straightened a few things out and showed me what's possible. For that, I am forever grateful.

Nowadays, I don't feel lost anywhere. Even if I feel out of place, I know where I am: in my body. Years of not being able to set down roots helps you stay unattached to anyone, anything, or any outcome. Raising my baseline has taught me to expect new things and expect better things to keep coming. Finally, I have stopped wandering around lost, and instead have stayed connected to who I know I am. Dean and I had this engraved compass in the shape of a heart that read, "love will find the way." For a while, when one of us would travel, we would take the talisman to find our way back home. I no longer need a talisman to find my way anywhere. I know I can always find my way if I follow my heart.

Chapter 9
Silent Screams

When I started sharing that I'd be writing a book, many people asked about what inspired it. There are a few pivotal points in my life that solidified the need to write a book, however, this has been a forty-four year process. I can't tell you exactly when this book started, besides at my birth. As I've shared, I have been wanting to write this memoir for a long time, but I realized that if I waited until I thought I was smart enough, skilled enough, or influential enough, I might make it to my grave without ever writing it.

This goes for all of us. If we wait till we feel 'ready,' that day will never come. I wrote this book through my small Self chattering away. I would write a chapter and when I went to reread it the next day, I would harshly criticize what I had come up with. I would see all the holes, errors, and disjointed stories and want to just hit delete. A word of advice to any aspiring author: *never hit delete!*

If your small Self could run your life, which it often does, it would constantly delete any and all progress you ever consider making. Trust me, I only know this from experience. Yes, I finally arrived at a point where

I have written my memoir *and* it is about a decade 'late' by my expectations. This is because I let my small Self intimidate me.

This happened for years in all areas of my life. The first time I ever considered writing a book was after I picked up my first self-development book from the library while I was still staying in the shelter. There I was, a homeless, single mother with no job or promising future, renting a personal development book. The voice in my head just laughed and yelled and criticized me for even thinking my life could get any better than it was; that *I* could become any better than I was.

I call that voice the small Self now, but honestly, she was just a straight-up bitch. She was rude and crude and never held back a single nasty thought or statement. I felt like any time I attempted to take a step forward, she would yank me back by my hair. I struggled with her silently for decades and she ran my life during that time.

Oddly enough, there was still an urge from my heart that would cause me to rent those books and read them anyway. I would read words of encouragement while that inner bitch screamed "YOU'RE NO GOOD! Give it up Simi, you're nothing. You're trash! You'll never live up to anything. That book is worthless to you. Give up."

Give up. She would constantly tell me to give up and finally, one day, I screamed back, "NO, *YOU* GIVE IT UP! I am never quitting! I refuse to give up. I will never quit on my dreams!" and she shut up...for about ten minutes.

You see, my friend, that small Self will always be around. The desire of that part of you is to stay safe and comfortable. That part of you is not interested in risk-taking. It is interested in looking good and sticking with what is familiar, even if what is predictable is also miserable.

My small Self loved the women's shelter. It was safe, predictable, and by definition, sheltered me. In my heart, I was miserable. In my head, I was safe, and this created a storm within me. I was constantly at war with myself.

"Go for it."

"No, don't"

"GO FOR IT!"

"No! We can't!"

This tug of war was nauseating and exhausting. So exhausting that things I wished would have taken me days and weeks took me months and years. Of course, my inner bitch loved to tease me about that, too. This battle wore me down time and time again, until I realized it wasn't each specific circumstance that created the lesson, it was the fight with my small Self that I had to master. Over time, I set boundaries with my small Self. She is allowed in my car, but I'm the driver. Sometimes she is next to me while driving, sometimes she's in the back seat, and sometimes she gets in the trunk. I decide, I'm the driver.

When I left my marriage and went to the shelter, I thought I was facing the truths of life but still felt like I was in hiding. This didn't really feel like handling my problems. The only difference I could see was that I went from relying on Fred to relying on the shelter's support. This was the weak spot that that inner voice could use to overtake me and make me believe what a loser I was. Back then, I didn't exactly have the perspective that I was truly making progress. Even when I had glimpses of progress, it never felt like enough. The skill of perspective takes practice to master and utilize, and I am strengthening that skill to this day.

The skill to master shifting perspective should be made a subject in school for every person. There was no schooling that really prepared me to be an author. There wasn't a specific lesson, relationship, or success that made me feel valid and ready. It has been a constant creation of who I am to become a woman who can put a book together and share these incredible memories, stories, and lessons with you. During the writing process, I still had to have a few battles with the small Self to finish it. I had to move past imposter syndrome and past questioning my abilities to connect with a publisher and get it to print. This wasn't a process of learned skill. It was a process of practiced self-acceptance, determination, commitment, and resilience.

In line with the same topic, becoming the first immigrant in my ESL program to earn her GED was a time when I had to work beyond the voice of that inner bitch to achieve something great. I was collecting all of the material evidence that would prove that I could and was capable. I loved proving her wrong. She had nothing nice to say when I sat down for that test, and she was *dead* wrong. I passed that exam with flying colors, and all of my instructors were so proud of me.

"Congrats," she scoffed. "You were *someone* in Romania with a career and status. You already have a high school diploma and higher education from two universities and you are earning your US high school accreditation at the age of thirty-four, loser." She really never quit. She put a huge damper on most of my life experiences, good and bad. At one point, I finally detached from what she had to say when I recognized whose voice she was.

In 2015, I took a trip for a visit back to Romania. My dad had passed a year before, in September, and I couldn't go to his funeral because I didn't have my green card yet. Without the green card, you can leave the country but you can't come back. I finally got mine two months after my dad passed. After six years of being gone, it was time to plan the trip to Romania. We went back for my niece's eighteenth birthday party, which is a big deal in Romania. Looking back, honestly, it felt more like an unspoken promise being fulfilled. I always knew in my heart that if I wanted to visit my family, I would have to be the one to go back and visit, because I was the one who left.

Planning that trip was an emotionally charged experience. My dad was not with us anymore, seeing everyone again was difficult, giving my niece the surprise gift of showing up at her party, and bringing Dean, my American boyfriend, with me, all contributed to an emotional visit. It was a roller coaster, but I had no idea how important it would become to my growth and evolution.

When I went back with Dean and Andrei, I was in a comfortable position in my life. I was making good money, in a healthy relationship, and was pretty successful overall. I was feeling the best I had ever felt and figured going back home would be a good experience for the three of us. One thing I can say for certain is that it wasn't a great trip for that small Self.

When I went back to see the same people and hear them talking about the same things as when I left six years prior, I knew that I was different. So different, in fact, that when people started saying to me "you've changed" I took it as a complete compliment, even if it wasn't intended as such. A smaller, more insecure version of me would have been concerned with other people's opinions of me. The new me that went back to Romania that year was a woman who knew herself on a whole new level. I was living a life in America where no one called me names, bullied me, or told me how to live my life. It was upsetting to go back and hear friends and family having so many opinions about my life. They were the same people who didn't care what I had been going through for the past six years.

Hearing voices outside of me judge or doubt me helped me identify where that inner bitch originated. I have received criticism from so many directions my entire life. For the first time, it occurred to me that the voice in my head wasn't sourced from within. I saw it as a collection of voices, and none of them belonged to me. This created space in my mind for me to sense who I might be without that voice, or at least imagine if I dialed her volume down.

The 'me' that emerged on that trip to Romania didn't feel lost, confused, or unworthy. She didn't question how she was doing in life. She stared at her past, which had not changed, and stood in contrast to everything she once knew. This is when that inner bitch really lost her grip on me. So no matter what she has to say, how often she speaks up, or how loudly she screams, she can never run my life again. She can never be the driver again. I fired her from the executive position on that trip and after that, I started firing words that she would use to try to scare me out of my greatness. I also learned that the responsibility of going back just because I was the one who left was not my belief anymore. I made it clear that I had no reason to go back and everyone was welcome to visit us in the US. It was the same distance either way.

While visiting my family, I had to make peace with who and how they were, without judgment. Growing up in Romania, judgment was all I knew. In my time in America, my relationship with judgment shifted. I had been discriminated against in so many ways that I realized prejudices served no one. So, while there was a part of me that wished they were different, instead of trying to change or fix them, I finally accepted them. I quit trying to make everyone understand where I was at in my life. I finally understood that maybe, they couldn't even comprehend that world, and decided that I didn't have to explain anything to anyone. We are just different people living in two different worlds and I have learned to be okay with that.

I was able to board my flight home to America with peace in my heart and silence in my mind; two of the most rewarding things that no amount of money can buy. No more judgment. No more justifying or fighting back. No more failed expectations or guilt trips. No more doubting, questioning, or second guessing. I was officially no longer the woman who fled Romania to escape. I boarded that flight back to America as a woman with power and choice. From then on, I chose to love myself.

I solidified within myself that I was the one with the say in my life. Even in my loving relationship with Dean, I appreciated the way he respected the space I required, which gave me room to take ownership over my life, as well as the direction of it. Our trip to Romania brought us closer together when he had the opportunity to see where I came from and who I have become along my journey.

The time in my life that my inner bitch had her death grip around my neck was my time in the shelter. Those personal development books helped, but damn, she was strong. Something really interesting was happening during that time of my life. I had the drastically opposing encouragement of the books and shelter employees saying "you can do it!" and my inner bitch shouting "yeah fuckin' right!"

I chose to follow the encouragement, and this led to something that still blows me away to this day. As I prepared to write this book, I started to do some self studying. I pulled out all of my old notebooks, flash cards, and diaries to get back in touch with the different versions of myself, and revisit those phases of my life.

Even as I write this, I am re-amazed at what I found. When I was in the shelter, my first diary read all of the things that I have, and am. Back then, I thought it was ego-centric when I would write "I want to be famous," but it was a driving factor that kept me going during that time. Call it whatever you want, it pushed me to get me out of that shelter and take steps toward a better life.

I wrote down full descriptions of my future on flash cards. My books, my success, my speaking career, and traveling all over the world. When reviewing my flash cards and diaries, I recalled how scared I was of my own visions. I would have these big, lofty daydreams and it would immediately cause panic within me. "Who do you think you are!?" my small Self would shout.

Those flash cards were my biggest secret. I hid them so that other people couldn't find them and label me as 'certified crazy.' I felt as though I had no right to dream that big, but I could imagine celebrities sitting in my house and having regular conversations over coffee. I could see myself on stages. I could see it, but I couldn't exactly sense it. Even if you asked me if I believed in manifestation back then, I would have laughed at you. I didn't believe in any of that shit and neither did that inner bitch; at least there was *something* that we agreed on.

But as I mentioned, something interesting was happening in my life back then. The more I focused on the empowerment end of the spectrum, the more empowered I became. This certainly didn't happen overnight, but years later, I can see how it eventually did. I shifted from simple flash cards to feelings of empowerment. Empowerment turned into self-encouragement and that turned my day-dreaming into declaring and claiming my future.

Even though I didn't feel empowered consistently, I was still writing those poems that seemed to be my future self encouraging me. Reading this poem now gives me chills. The internal battle was so real, and such a struggle. I am just happy to see that the stronger version of me won over my small Self of the past.

My road

There were so many shadows
Brought darkness in my life
Is my time now to follow
The heavy road to light

I turned into this street
And recognized a face,
It looked at me so pleased:
'You know me! I'm your Past!"

I felt my blood start boiling
My body shook so bad,
But tried to stay calm, knowing
That won't help me to get mad.

It said: "Let's take a walk together,
We went through so much, once…"
"That's right, so you know better,
In you I will never trust!"

I saw its tears, rolling
But, didn't impress me;
"You need to cut that, Honey
Are fake, always you'll be!"

"I know you for too long,
Can't fool me, anymore!
It's my time to move on,
You can't be on my road!"

Past stood behind me, staring
At me, walking away
I didn't let time wasting
It's nothing else to say.

It's hard and is confusing
I've never been like this
But I will keep on going
The Past I'll never miss.

The Future is my friend
In this challenging trip
And I'll do nothing bad
Believing in my dreams

They make my road more easy
And build my confidence
I'm free now to get busy
To work for happiness.

I think it is so important to understand the power of writing down your
dreams, visions, and goals. I spoke my future into my reality by writing it
down. I didn't always believe in my dreams, but I could see them clearly
and am grateful to my past self for writing them all down. I am not sure I

would believe myself otherwise. Some days, I just sit back and laugh to myself in amazement, "Who could've thought that this is exactly what I would be helping my clients with these days. Who could've thought that this would become my career?"

There are plenty of scientific studies to validate that writing down a goal dramatically increases the likelihood of achieving that goal. I enjoy sharing this with my clients because if we are vague, unclear, or indirect about what we desire, we will have lackluster results. Someone smarter than me once said, "If you don't know where you are going, you end up exactly there." That stuck with me. It taught me to be clear, direct, and specific. If we took ourselves and our manifestation skills more seriously, we would declare more specific dreams with more purpose and intention. I hope that you learn from this book to become more serious about your creative power. You are the creator of your life.

No matter what your spiritual or religious background might be, I will reference some type of higher power, some source or force that moves us when we are weak and that pushes us when we think we can't take another step further. Although we may not feel very spiritual or enlightened all of the time, going for big dreams is by nature, an inspired action or an action in spirit. The nature of being inspired is being moved by spirit.

I believe in this spirit because it freaks me out who the heck I was when I wrote such clear descriptions of the life that I am currently living back when I was living in that shelter. I certainly didn't feel empowered then, yet, there was a small part of me that knew where I was headed.

At that time, the words on those flash cards were not my beliefs at all. I was *not* someone who thought that way, I was someone who believed she didn't deserve the kind of life I was writing down. I would think, "This lifestyle is not for a homeless, non-English speaking, undocumented person like me." Yet, for some reason, I wrote it all down.

I kept wanting to believe what I was writing. I was willing to believe, but I had very little faith, so I was making statements that I wasn't really sure would come true. Now, I have an amazing new life that I declared years ago! I wrote it down with so much detail and description that it blows my f'king mind. Unbelievable! This is my experience of a divine download. These visions were truly inspired because I was not a woman who believed. If I would have stopped when I thought I knew who I was, I would have never gotten to where I am.

Who you are, who you *think* you are, is temporary. Everything is temporary: the good, the bad, the ugly, the indifferent. It's all temporary.

In the next chapter, I am going to share about the impermanence of life. Throughout my experiences, I have watched so many things, people, places, and situations come and go. When I got too attached, I would experience more pain. To this day, I still have people ask me when I am going to put roots down somewhere. For a long time I felt guilty about this, like something was wrong with me. We kept moving like gypsies and never settled. Now I know that I don't want to settle. I don't want to put my roots anywhere. That is not the life I choose for myself. That is not my belief. I'm choosing a different lifestyle that allows me to travel anywhere, at any time, and that is exactly what I am creating.

When I accepted the truth that everything is generally temporary, I could see when a season was ending and I could better practice letting go. Accepting the impermanence of problems *and successes* will help us a great deal emotionally. It provides the clarity to keep raising our voices, standards, vibes, and expectations, and continuously put one foot in front of the other to go for all that is possible and available in this lifetime.

You have a great gift and it is yours to deliver, but it will require you going far beyond any recognizable comfort zone to fulfill your life's purpose. There is no going back to where you started. Every next level takes you further than you have ever been. Just like when I stood in my new apartment in LA and my small Self said "starting over," I knew I would never be starting over from where I originally began. So, you heard it here first! The term 'starting over' is officially fired! There's no such thing as square one. We are never the same as when we started. It might look like I'm starting over, I might be at the same point, *but* I am on a higher lever on my evolutional spiral; I have upleveled.

I will continue to walk you through this process and show you how you can declare your future too. I understand what it feels like to struggle with faith but you have to take the chance of believing that you can manifest what you can see for yourself. In order to do so, you will have to notice and release the voice of your inner critic. You must be willing to let go of your sexy excuses and upgrade your limiting beliefs.

Another journal entry I found in my notebooks was a list I made about what I was ready to release: embarrassment, disappointment, guilt, sadness, loneliness, and feeling lost, scared, hurt, and angry. I wrote about letting go of the things I realized were holding me back. It was really the first time that I sat down to identify my emotions and feelings. It was the first time that I became curious about how many I have, know, feel, etc.

Releasing doubts created space for something new as my confidence slowly increased. In the beginning of this book, I shared about the feeling of freedom. Sometimes I back up and just ask nobody, "Really?!?" I am here. I am where I imagined myself so many years ago. Years ago, when I wasn't sure if what I was saying could be true and yet, here I am. I used to imagine my life like what I would see in the movies, and now, I'm actually living it.

Something else that I had written on a flash card was: "Respect is differential. You belong to yourself. You belong to no one. Differentiation is essential." Being respected was a big deal for me and I dissected the meaning of respect as deeply as I could. I had to take an honest look at my pride versus my shame, and understand the meaning of it. When I originally wrote that flash card, I also had the fearful thoughts of, "Who would ever respect me again if they found out about my experience? I'm not proud of where I am. How can I ever be proud about myself after this experience?"

Because I was able to differentiate and disassociate from that nasty inner bitch and tell my small Self to take a back seat, the silent screams ceased. They stopped ringing in my ears and I could hear again. I could sense the whispers of my heart telling me about my potential and giving me the inspiration to go forward boldly. Did I truly believe what I was hearing from my heart? Hell no, but I knew it was possible, and I was willing and committed to try to make it a reality.

I did the work and the healing. I cleaned up and updated my limiting beliefs. It took a decade, and now I am proud and honored to be able to share my life through a memoir. This is not about stacking words, phrases, and pages together; it is about the journey that got me here. I am not you and you are not me. We may have had different experiences in life but I know that we can relate on the heart level. In fact, while we're at it, I should mention that the phrase "I've been in your shoes" is fired too. I haven't been in your shoes. I haven't walked your path and you haven't walked mine. No two life experiences are the same, and I respect that. What I know and understand are the emotions and feelings you've experienced. As humans, we know heartbreak, shame, anger, tragedy, and pain, in a way that gives us access to each other. Some of us know abandonment, abuse, and neglect more than others. Many of us know joy, play, laughter, and celebration, as well. This is what ties us together beyond our nationalities, beliefs, or desires. It is when we speak up and share who and where we have been that the screaming can stop.

Sharing my story has been a healing process all on its own. It has resurfaced memories that I have not otherwise revisited and helped me process energy that has been stored in my body. Sharing is healing. Speaking up is setting yourself free. I wrote this book for me. I published it for you. You sit where you are with this book in your hand. The words on these pages have been born straight from my inspired heart, through my fingertips, straight to you and yours. My intention, hope, prayer, and commitment with this book is that it shines light into the vast world of possibility. I aim to inspire you to take a look at your own journey and see the way it has shaped, refined, and redefined who you know yourself to be.

Chapter 10

My Own Personal Hell

If there is one thing that has stuck with me from my heritage, it is guilt, shame, blame, and self-hatred. Of all the things that have happened to me, there were many days that I was the worst thing happening to me. I was so unkind to myself. I was tough, harsh, and judgmental. So much of my identity was wrapped up in self-hatred. I judged my body, my decisions, my life: all of it. It was all fair game for my inner bitch, and this felt like my own personal hell.

I used to call the shelter 'a playground for victimhood.' The counselors and volunteers protected you from taking responsibility for your situation. "It's not your fault," they would encourage gently, and it would just make me cringe. My Romanian background made me want to take responsibility for the experience. I resented myself for the position I was in and punished myself with harsh words and cigarettes. I felt like a waste so I didn't care for my body. I ate like shit and felt like shit. I felt dumb, stupid, and embarrassed. I insisted it was my fault and that I deserved what happened, and so I refused to give myself any grace.

I started smoking in high school. It was one of the only ways I knew how to handle stress and I smoked like a chimney through some of the most stressful times of my life. It was such a weird feeling to know I was harming my body with cigarettes, yet continuing because I thought I deserved some kind of punishment. I would look at that little cancer stick in my hands and watch the smoke float out of my mouth and loved and hated it at the same time. I knew they were terrible for me but I felt like a terrible person. This somehow justified my habit for a long time.

Speaking of a long time, over the course of my life, the concept of time has been absolutely demolished. Thinking back about our time in the shelter feels like it was a hundred years ago. Months seemed like years, certain nights felt like an eternity, and yet, some memories still feel like they were just yesterday. It's funny how the mind does that, but something I will never forget is 'the wait.'

The *constant* waiting: getting out of the shelter, trying to obtain my authorization for work, my green card, my citizenship. It took eight years from the time I arrived in America to the day that I received my citizenship. The wait of that was excruciating. I was living in hell on Earth waiting for other people and processes to work themselves out. I was so limited in what I could do before I just had to wait again.

I will never forget when I was awaiting mail from Homeland Security, and I was sure the women in the shelter were sick of me asking if I had any mail, twice a day. My inner critic never stopped this whole time. "Oh my God, Simona. You are so annoying! Just stop. Give up!" But, I never gave up. I just kept asking.

The patience that I have had to practice over the course of my life has been like pulling out all of my teeth, one at a time. I've never considered myself a very patient person and all that waiting had certainly been a special kind of hell. A work visa only lasts for one year, and since I hadn't received residency that year, I had to continuously reapply for the visa. I reapplied four years in a row before ever qualifying for the residency green card. I had been waiting to feel settled for so long that I actually forgot how long I had been waiting.

Another aspect of my own personal hell has been feeling like there is nowhere on this planet that I really belong. Sometimes, I would get so wrapped up in this feeling that I would sense myself feeling forgotten and lost in darkness. It would take my breath away and I would try so desperately to find something to hold onto.

This drove my desire to acquire my citizenship. I never felt at home in my own country. I didn't feel safe in relationships. So often, I felt alone and on my own. I am grateful for the people that showed up for me along my journey but when I would lay my head on my pillow at night during those dark times, I would question everything.

I remember the day when we completed Andrei's application for his US passport. To celebrate, my friend, Carlota, had Andrei and I over for dinner, and she handed me a gift to celebrate the moment Andrei and I were both recognized as US citizens. When I opened my gift, it was a coffee mug that read PATIENCE across the front in pink letters. I laughed at the irony and told her I had none. I will never forget the way she gently smiled at me and softly said, "eight years, Simona. You have been waiting eight years for this. You *have* patience."

Her reflection opened up a place in my heart that I didn't know I had. "I guess that I do have patience," I thought to myself. "I also have resilience, faith, and commitment," and it was finally time to accept and allow it fully. This moment marked a time in which I allowed myself to start being kinder to myself. I had gone through the entire process to gain citizenship because it is what *I* wanted. I went further than most and that takes courage, faith, and a lot of patience. I started to realize I wasn't so bad, after all.

This whole process shaped me in ways I did not understand until pretty recently. It is impossible to think of planting roots or calling a place 'home' when your status there is so impermanent. Throughout the eight years of acquiring my citizenship, everything always felt so temporary: my place of living, my relationships, my work, everything, I did not realize how this conditioned me to become unattached from things, people, and outcomes. It never felt good at the time. Most days, it felt downright scary. However, this is a true advantage to me now.

I have come to understand the Law of Impermanence. This is traditionally a Buddhist belief and practice. However, I think that many Western civilizations are not taught enough about this natural law of order. The concept of this law is that everything comes and goes. Nothing lasts forever. All we have is the present moment. This isn't a sad truth, but just a truth. It is a truth we would all be better off with if we understood it more deeply and accepted it more widely.

I will share bits and pieces about the Law of Impermanence as we go on, to offer you the opportunity to release anything that you feel you hold onto. This law has been such a blessing to me because I can remember that bad times don't last. This helps me move through them with more clarity and confidence. This also reminds me that good times don't last. This encourages me to appreciate when things are going well and to really take it all in. When we can live detached, we have a new level of freedom that no status can grant us. When we can go with the flow of impermanence, we are freed up to enjoy the ride.

Without this awareness, we hold onto so many things that limit us.

Our attachments limit us. Our beliefs about the rules limit is. Our perceived identities limit us.

To buy into 'the way things are' is what keeps us stuck in place and prevents us from living a life of possibility. This can stop us in so many ways and limit what we can create and offer to the world. The way I used to talk to myself and identify with being a 'worthless, piece of shit' completely limited me from being how great I actually am. I have always been great but I haven't always believed it. I had to stop being so downright mean to myself to escape the hell I was creating for myself.

When I began to raise my vibe, I improved my self-talk. I stopped smoking. I cut back on cursing. I started believing in myself and my potential. I wanted to feel good more than I wanted to be right about my belief that I was stupid or undeserving. I learned to apply the Law of Impermanence to my identity and way of being. If nothing lasted forever, then it was time to let my limiting beliefs go.

This is an invitation to let go of your own limiting ways. What would become possible for you if you decided that instead of worthless or unworthy, you are a risk-taker who is willing to go for things beyond what the eye can see. What would you go for? What would you create?

I had no idea that I would achieve the things I had written in those flash cards so many years ago, and here I am having manifested so much of it. We can speak our lives into truth. We can speak things into existence, and a force greater than us is behind us: supporting, guiding, protecting, providing for us. It will show up in this physical world in many shapes and forms but we must be on the lookout for its guidance.

I was able to exit my own personal hell by letting it be temporary. Once I found my way out, I knew there would be no going back. I knew too much to ever go back there. Even if I stumbled upon misfortune, I was not the same hellish woman degrading herself into misery. Raising my voice also meant elevating my language to the frequency of kindness, compassion, and love. If I wouldn't talk to someone else that way, I wouldn't talk to myself that way. That doesn't mean that I'm not visited by old ways of being every now and then. I am. I do have moments when I feel sorry for myself, judge myself, and even others. They are moments in which I choose to stop, release, and rise above, because like never before, I believe in possibility and expansion for myself and for others. I believe in everyone being capable and deserving of a better life.

The same way I could speak hell into existence is the same way I can speak heaven into existence. We all have this capability and power. It is time we use our power to create more good in the world. This is how we can change the world, individual by individual, showing up with more kindness, compassion, and love.

Paper Never Forgets!

Write down your insights.

Part 3

Sparks of Light

Chapter 11

Earth Angels

More good was brought into my world directly through the hands and hearts of a few specific people worth mentioning. These people seemed to be sent straight from the heavens at some of my darkest hours. There have been so many random acts of kindness throughout my life that often didn't make sense to me. The only sense I could make of the timing that some of the help that has arrived in my life is 'divine intervention;' that a force greater than me sent direct and indirect help to pave the path forward.

This wasn't always easy to accept. As mentioned, my inner voice was critical about how much I needed the help of others. I felt weak and I accepted help because I felt like I had no other option, but my relationship to kindness was transactional; if someone was generous to you, it came at a cost.

This belief stemmed from my upbringing, because the people around me always seemed to keep score of their generosity. Not only did this feel gross, it stopped me from wanting to accept help, so I became conditioned to turning it down. In America, that seemed different. People were just more kind, more often. They were more genuinely generous.

I felt that people like May and Catherine didn't owe me anything and yet, gave me everything. Even though I needed what they were offering me, I was still hesitant to accept their support at first. I wasn't sure what I would have to do or give in return. Over time, accepting that some people just know to do the right thing helped me relax about receiving help. I didn't understand what it meant to just give without expectation until I moved to America. I finally learned that we can give and receive help just because we want to, and most importantly, not *to* or *from* the same people. I finally understood the concept of *paying it forward*, and adopted it into my belief system.

Even more people like Macy and Catherine entered my life, and we all seemed to cross paths naturally. I knew deep down that a Higher Power was protecting us, guiding us, and leading us to each other. For example, the shelter volunteers, like Ms. Daryl, who taught me about the power of volunteering, and Miss Anne, who supported me in finding and identifying my emotions. They saw me through my restoration. Ms. Opal, my divorce attorney, who made sure I had two officers by me on my day in court to feel safe, just in case Fred showed up. She set me free. There were others, like my friend Tatiana from Romania, who housed us and made us part of her family, and my amazing boss, Tammie, who gave me my first job with no interview. She saw me for my potential behind the simple clothes and broken English. Then, there was my landlord in Minnesota, Jarett, who trusted me enough to sign a lease before I got my job, with no credit score, and no SS. His trust was just based on "I have a good feeling about you." He was always looking out for me, giving me upgrades to the newest apartment available, and making me feel so taken care of.

There are many more Earth Angels who have blessed me along my journey and walked with me along the way. I will share a few more in the second half of this book, like my three chosen sisters, Cassandra, Kenni, and Jeanette. In the years of becoming an entrepreneur and leader, there were programs and opportunities that moved me forward greatly. I have had coaches and mentors who helped me identify, accept, and release the hidden parts of myself. There were many colleagues and networks that have led me to where I am today. For all of these, I am forever grateful.

This includes my first husband, Sorin, who was my first love. He gave me Andrei, and our divorce uprooted me in a way that made me ready to move to the US. Regardless of the pain of a broken heart, ending our marriage forced me to look in a different direction across the Atlantic Ocean, so now I get to celebrate that divorce. Same goes for my second husband, Fred. He certainly didn't always seem like an Angel and my time with him often felt like hell, but he was a part of my journey that has made me who I am today.

Fred prepared me for an eight year immigration battle and helped me see exactly how resilient I am. I believe that even the ones who challenge us greatly have been sent from that same source to further shape and refine us. There are other trying times I will share that have really altered the direction of my life. There are plenty more trials that caused me to raise my voice and create the platform I stand on today.

I also had Dean, who shared his life with me for seven years. He showed me life beyond what I could imagine for myself. I will share more about our relationship and its end in later chapters, but the difference he has made for me will always last. He showed up right when I decided I didn't need a man in my life to feel whole. I believe loving myself is, in fact, what called him in. It was a relationship of two independent people actively choosing each other. Life with Dean elevated my experience of love and will forever matter greatly to me.

There is of course Andrei, who has helped me grow from the inside out. This young man has taught me as much as any of my adventures. He is wise beyond his years, and intuitive. Anything you have read about me, you can pretty much imagine that Andrei was by my side having his own experience in the situation. I have not always been proud of that fact, but I have done everything within my power to care for him and give him the best chance at a great life that I could. I am honored to be his Momma and proud to call him my son. He is my inspiration, my teacher.

All of these amazing Earth Angels have showed up to guide me where I am meant to go. Knowing this, I can sense when it is my turn to meet people where they are and support their journey as well. This has led me to my work in helping parents, children, families, leaders, and more. Being an Earth Angel for others is a gift and honor as well. We all have this duty. This is a Collective effort to love and help each other, and important in what we are all creating. Like anything else, relationships too are impermanent. Some are short, some are long, some are life-long. I believe that everyone walks into our lives to serve a specific purpose, and when that purpose is complete, the relationship is over. It is nobody's fault, there is no right or wrong, the "work" has been completed. To trust and believe that we are being moved forward together and supporting each other is absolutely essential in us fulfilling our greatest purposes.

No one of us is meant to be the highest of all. We are all meant to be the greatest we can be at what we do, so that we may experience ourselves as a contribution to humanity. This allows us to appreciate each other for the gifts that we all came to deliver, so that we may depend on each other, count on each other, and raise each other up; especially when we forget who we are and what we are here to do. Even though this book is called "Raising *my* Voice" it is about each of us raising our *own* voice and believing in the goodness of one another. It is our duty to support each other and raise our own voices to create harmony in this world.

I understand this can be a challenge because we aren't always present to the potential of how harmonious life can be. It is sometimes missing from our own hearts and minds. For me, some of my inner turmoil occurred when I was not connected to a higher power. I felt very alone and on my own when I felt spiritually disconnected. In fact, spirituality was something that was irrelevant for me, until it wasn't.

I was baptized and raised Orthodox, and throughout my childhood, I was forced to go to church. I had no interest in it. I never understood what we were doing, and I certainly never understood the way we had to dress up. The way people looked mattered so much more than how they acted. Everything felt so judgmental. The basic rule I understood was, if you were good, you'd go to Heaven. If you were bad, you'd go to Hell. I was confused about people that I knew were bad, but would go to church on Sunday to be forgiven and go home to be bad again. As a child, it made me question everything I was being told. I would wonder, "So you get to be bad, but if you go to church, all is forgiven?" It didn't make sense and nobody could help me understand it.

There were so many ridiculous rules about what would send us to Heaven or Hell, but none of them seemed to make sense to me. What also didn't make sense to me is how mean, critical, or rude someone could be and still be considered as going to heaven. It seemed that if it was in the name of God, it was okay. But it didn't really seem that God was the judge in my world, people were. If you didn't do what the people said was good and right, then you were bad and wrong. The overused phrase "do what the priest says, not what the priest does," was pretty hard for a child to follow.

I never believed in any of this and couldn't wait to get out. I vividly remember my last day of being Orthodox. I had to get Andrei baptized for the sake of cultural pressures. I knew I was just doing what was expected of me but it would be the last religious expectation I ever met. I had to argue with the priest to be allowed into the church simply because according to the man-made rules of this religion, I was considered 'not clean' because I had just recently had a baby. "I'm not *clean*?" I wondered. Is this how all baptisms go? Are all mothers shamed about reproducing because it meant we had sex? This infuriated me.

I was not considered 'clean' enough to even enter the church until the priest prayed above my head while I was kneeling. All I could think was, "if God 'blessed me with a child' then why would God look at me like I'm *dirty*?" I could hardly see or speak through my anger, so I didn't. The whole ceremony, I was in the corner, by myself, watching friends and family being a part of my child's ceremony, which I was not allowed to be part of. I watched from a distance as though I had been shunned. I felt like a sinner; dirty, punished. It was the last straw for me. Before the water was dry on little baby Andrei's body, I turned to the priest the moment after he had baptized my son and said, "you will never see me here again," and I left for good.

The day I walked out of those doors was the day that I walked into the next phase of my life. It was liberating to raise my voice and take a stand against something I didn't believe in. I had had many debates about our religion, especially with my dad, but I hadn't spoken up or stood up for myself in this way till that day. The first time being the last time was enough for me.

I have made it pretty clear that I don't exactly claim any specific path of spirituality. Although Buddhist traditions and beliefs seem to make the most sense to me right now, I can't even say that that will be true for me in ten years, or maybe even ten minutes from now. I am fine with remaining open to what that greater force might be or represent.

One thing I can tell you about is the most spiritual experience I've ever had. It was in February of 2019 when Dean and I were visiting Egypt. He had a conference to attend and I came along for the trip. I loved traveling the world and took every opportunity I could by myself and with Dean.

In a coaching training program that I completed, we had to do an exercise in which we listed all of our priorities. We had to list them in order of importance, and spirituality was the very last on my list. I had fully avoided this breakthrough for many years because I never felt connected to religion or spirituality or some higher power. However, at this point, there have been too many things that have happened in my life that only make spiritual sense. So, I'm not always sure what I believe in, but I do believe in some force greater than us.

I remembered not liking the atmosphere in Egypt. The men holding guns and searching the taxi car at the entry of the hotel, who were there "for my safety" made me instantly feel unsafe. I was thinking "If this were a safe place, we wouldn't need protection, right?" I felt very uncomfortable for being a white woman not of their culture. I remember feeling violated by the way I was being looked at by the men there. I was uncomfortable with the gazes I was getting and I was even more uncomfortable with the hundred-plus degree heat. Due to the temperature, my outfit was accordingly, hot summer day clothing. In reaction to the looks, I wanted to put many layers on, so as to not be seen. And so I did, leggings under my dress, a sweater and scarf to cover my bare hands; I traded comfort for more clothing.

We had done a few things together on our trip, but while Dean made his way to the conference, I took the opportunity to get a tour of the Grand Pyramid. As it is an ancient structure, there are many rules about being there, such as not touching the walls, no photography indoors, no wandering off the path, and so on. As uncomfortable as I was in Egypt, walking around the Grand Pyramid was a completely different experience. I felt my mind, my heart, my soul, my whole being expanding along with the massive blocks of Pyramids and endless spaciousness of the Sahara Desert.

It was as if I immediately entered a new place in the world, another dimension, even. I was no longer in Egypt. My surroundings quickly shifted from fast, loud, and hot, to slow and serene. I specifically remember the drop in temperature. One hundred plus degrees in Egypt had no effect on the thick structure of the pyramid. It dropped to seventy degrees inside and calmed me down in an instant. I remember feeling this cold air wash over me and cause a wave of relief.

I was in these ancient, sacred ruins surrounded in peace. I felt so calm. I felt so guided. The contrast from outside these walls was so mysterious to me, but the way that I felt led and protected in here made me more than willing to trust it.

As we began our tour, I remember ducking and squeezing through little tunnels to get to stairwells to climb higher and higher. While stepping up a stair, I looked up toward the ceiling, which was far and narrow. When we approached the top chamber, I remember walking around, slowly observing it all, and feeling so much. This indescribable, overwhelming feeling rushed over me. I wasn't sure what I was sensing but it was so powerful that it brought me to tears. I simply remember being in there crying and releasing. There was such an exaggerated feeling of contraction and expansion in my chest with every breath. With each inhale and exhale, I felt calmer, more peaceful, and connected. The man who supervised the tourists in that room noticed and approached me to check up and ask if I was okay. Honestly, I wasn't actually sure if I was okay, but I let him know that nothing was wrong.

Discreetly, he offered to take my picture to remember this very precious moment. I knew it was against the rules and I was so grateful he was willing to do that for me. He told me he would leave me be and let me stay longer and catch up with the next group. I couldn't stop noticing how much peace had washed over me. In a sense, I felt 'home,' or like I had been in this place before. I had never felt this feeling but I didn't question it. I just felt it. I moved around that room for a while and made my way back down the stairs with a new group of tourists.

When I made my way to the bottom of the stairs, another tour guide offered to take my picture at the bottom. I was so grateful, yet so intrigued by what had encouraged two different people to make the same exception for me. After getting my second picture taken, I walked to the exit, where my guide anxiously approached me and asked me if I was okay. I reassured him that everything was fine. I told him that I felt at peace and grateful for the opportunity to stay up there for a few extra minutes beyond the regular twenty minute tour.

"My dear, that was two hours ago…" he said with confusion and worry. "I almost sent the medics up to check on you."

My eyes widened, my jaw dropped, and my heart sank. I couldn't understand what he said to me. Two hours? What I thought was twenty minutes was two hours? Does time measure differently inside of 4500-year-old construction? I had no idea how this could be but something divine had happened up there. Even to this day, I am still in search of exactly what happened up in the Grand Pyramid. As curious as I am about it, I don't question it, either. I knew I had made it 'home' in a way. It was the first time in my life that I felt a natural, spiritual sense of belonging. My soul recognized that place and it needed to be there on that day in that moment. I did not want to share this with Dean, and asked my guide to not worry him with it either. He will find out about this experience just like you, by reading this.

At the time, I didn't understand it myself and I couldn't explain it, so I definitely didn't want to worry him. I have a special person for this type of conversation, my chosen sister, Jeanette. Jeanette and I have a unique, energetic connection. She always calls me when I'm thinking of her and I always contact her when she is thinking of me. I know many people have this experience, but for us, it has worked every time, for years! When I shared my Egypt experience with her, she was not shocked. She was not shocked when I told her that my first earthquake in LA didnt scare me, I actually experienced calm and peace. My conversations with Jeanette about spirituality and energy work are as normal as any two friends talking about their grocery lists. It is one of the many reasons I love her so much and relate to her as a sister: a soul sister.

I still don't have a full explanation and frankly, I don't need it to believe that we are divinely guided, protected, cared for, and provided for. If you're willing to believe it, you will certainly be able to feel it. I believe that our guidance shows up through people, places, things, and opportunities, and we must keep our hearts open to receiving in order to identify the support when it shows up.

One major way that support and messages have shown up for me was through the self-help books in the shelter. Those books (or that experience) inspired me to write my own. I would love to invite you to join me in something that I do in my own life. As I write this book, I currently have the pages of forty other books open. Audiobooks really enable my process and obsession with books. I read or listen to a chapter here, a chapter there. I open up to a page or a quote of a physical book and I set it back down, leaving the bookmark in each so that I can catch back up with it when I'm ready, when it's the perfect time.

Whenever I finish a paperback book, I set it down along my travels. I leave it at the rental or the hotel. I leave it behind for the next person who it is meant to serve. When you finish this book, I invite you to share it with the next soul who is meant to read it. I invite you to co-create an impact with me; we are always stronger together than we are alone. If you love your own copy so much, I invite you to buy another and share it with the world. Certain books have gotten me where I am today. I have written this book to be a contribution to someone's journey.

My request to you is to help get this word out, raise your voice, raise my voice, and raise our Collective voice in order to help reach our human potential. So many people have contributed to my life by giving to me so generously, that I kindly request that you generously give out this book to inspire someone struggling in their own way. We have no idea how divine intervention will get to play a role in the life of whoever finds this gift.

Chapter 12
Open Borders Opened Up My Mind

There is this very familiar, surprised look I get from Americans when I casually share my history. People's eyes widen and their jaws drop when they learn more about where I came from. Growing up in Communist Romania was the most stereotypical situation you could imagine. I grew up with outdated traditions, gender roles, and family structures that people believe only existed over a hundred years ago. Having a fascination with Shakespeare, my son would compare my life to the playwright's, always questioning how my stories were indeed mine. While I'm not four hundred years old, there were boundaries and expectations set *for* us that we weren't given a choice about, and the truth is that they still exists today.

In reference to gender, sexuality, and lifestyle, men rule the roost, they are allowed to act how they want, and control the household. In many senses, women are property, expected to behave a certain, submissive way, and shamed if they do not. This traditionalism is rooted in a very basic, 'blue is for boys and pink is for girls' elementary type of mentality. I wish I could say this was generations ago but it is still very present, not only back in my country, but in so many other places in the world.

Beyond the family structure, the government ruled what was available to its population. The same way men were supreme, the government had control over everything, and did not allow room to question it, nor options to escape it. In fact, questions were not allowed, speaking up at all meant taking a risk to be locked up. It was as literal as "shut up or die." Back when I was young, growing up in the country, men wearing knives on their belts and 'going for the kill' was not unusual.

I used to eavesdrop on the adults' conversation after a wedding or big event to find out who had fought with who and who had stabbed who. I will never forget the day when I actually witnessed a man being stabbed. It was a holiday, and the whole village was out in the field celebrating with a picnic. Myself, my mom, and my dad were eating on the picnic blanket. My dad was talking with the mayor of the village who was standing next to our blanket.

Out of nowhere, he fell face down on our blanket, between us. To this day, I can still see the blood running from the open flesh on his back caused by a knife blade. He was stabbed in broad daylight, in front of everybody. He was stabbed by a man who had just been released from jail, who wanted revenge for being put there in first place.

My dad grabbed my mom's scarf, bandaged him tight, and rushed him to the medical center. Everyone was gossiping with everyone, sharing their opinions about what happened. Nobody paid any attention to what I and the other kids were exposed to. It was just another holiday, another stabbing. The violence was not a behavior that would be stopped, shamed, or discouraged. It was acceptable on a societal level for those 'who deserved it.'

In opposition to the Communist rule, there was significant national unrest and resistance in Europe as we approached the Romanian Revolution. As a people, we were so limited in what we could do, where we could go, and what we could attain, and as a result, the resistance was rising.

I was thirteen when The Romanian Revolution happened. I was young enough to not fully understand it all but old enough to comprehend the importance of it. What I was too young to understand was exactly how limited we were under a Communist government. It wasn't until President Ceauşescu was shot by his own people, which I still can't wrap my head around, that social and economic reform took place. It was then that I began to understand the limitations we all lived by. The fall of Communism ended the oppression that opened up Romania to the outside world.

The Revolution caused a lot of realizations for me. Most notably, the acknowledgment that I had no foundation to my education. I was already a country girl who had come to the city to study during middle school. I already felt so far beyond. Once we began adopting a democracy, I had the chance to learn about countries besides my own. I am not joking when I say that I had previously been so sheltered and uneducated that I thought the names of other places and countries were pretend, like fiction. The movies that we get to see, on weekends only, portrayed a lifestyle that to me was 'just in the movies.' Nobody ever told me that what I saw on limited TV time was actually real or possible. Just the gap between country lifestyle and city living was so big for me to understand that going beyond our borders was not even on my radar.

The opening of our borders opened up my mind. So many realities of the world were shut out by socialism. The Revolution busted down the barriers between the citizens of Romania and a world of liberation and possibility. I could say a seed of transformation had been planted within me at that time of my life. In some unknown way, this opening to the whole world coincided with me going to high school and opened me up for a new chapter in my life. It felt synchronized. I was amazed to find out that there was a *real* America and Asia. Of course I learned about it in geography classes, but this time was different. This time it was possible for people, not for me, but for others to actually go there. There were countries neighboring ours that we could actually visit, that we were allowed to visit. Not that I did, but this new potential caused me to start thinking far outside of everything I had ever known. It allowed my mind to expand beyond my circumstances, I began to dream, in hiding, but still, I started to dream!

The Romanian Revolution happened in 1989. My revolution, The Spark Revolution, began in 2017, and it caused a whole new level of upheaval and unrest. On October 31st, 2017, my son told me he had something he needed to share with me. He was visibly uncomfortable. I was concerned when he approached me because he looked more stressed than I'd ever seen before. After all we had been through, we had established that we could say anything to each other, so I was a bit nervous because I had no idea what he was about to tell me. Then, he came right out and said two words: "I'm gay."

I let out a sigh of relief that this was his news. Based on how tense he was, I was imagining that there was an emergency or something catastrophic had happened. I was grateful that everything was seemingly okay and we began to have a healthy, loving conversation about it.

I was amazed. The son who I had born and raised just busted down his own barriers to open up to me about his sexual orientation and identity. I was so grateful he felt safe to come out to me. It was not his moment of vulnerability that changed everything for me, it was during the conversation we had about it when I encouraged him to come out to his friends. When I told him it was safe to come out, Andrei asked me, "Mom? Did you ever have to come out as straight?" I felt a rush of embarrassment come over me.

This thought process had never occurred to me before. I have never had to come out as straight, or a woman, nor face any such pressure or stress. I was again re-amazed at my son's courage, but his question sent me spiraling into a whole new level of being lost. Somewhere deep down, I felt naturally prepared for this moment with my son. I realized that I had made a promise to love and guide him unconditionally and I wrote that promise out in this poem during my time in the shelter. I had no idea where life was taking us then and I had no idea where this moment would be taking us in the future. I just knew that wherever we were going, we'd be going together.

To My Son

Must be so hard for you
To understand all this
There is not the whole truth
Always is something missed

Sometimes I feel so hopeless
To guide you in this life
There is no book out there
To tell me what is right

I may have tried too hard
To teach you all the Good
But that's not the whole life
The Bad is part of it too

The innocence you have
Gives me the energy
To teach you the steps
On your walk to maturity

There are some rules in life
That don't apply the same
For every each of us
And this looks so unfair

I'm grateful for your trust
And know how hard you try
To follow my advice
Every day, all the time

I'm praying to the lord
To watch you all the time
This is my biggest goal
To have you save and smile

I promise you today
I will do all my best
To support you all the way
Ask anything, I'll say "yes"

Watching how fast you grow
And all the love you show me
Stop me from getting old
I feel just joy and happy

At this very moment, I had no idea what our future held. I was willing to trust our bond and faith to get us through the process. While I consider myself very accepting and progressive, I did not exactly have a very creative imagination in reference to this situation. Even though I have always considered myself to be inclusive, I realized that I had created a very traditional story for my son and his future. I realized my Romanian background reduced his life to one possible version of how things could go for him. When he shared his news with me, I realized that I had already made up in my head that he would meet a girl, have a family, and live out a heterosexual life.

Before this Revolution, my limited imagination created a very typical story for Andrei, which followed the stereotypical beliefs of a binary world. This was ironic because I used to face backlash for dressing him up in what society deemed to be "girls' clothing" or "girls' colors" because his wardrobe as a baby consisted of hand-me-downs from my niece. He wore lots of reds, pinks, flowers, and polka dots.

I hadn't realized that I had continued to project such a lack of options about my son's future. All his life, I had imagined my son bringing home some amazing, pretty, funny girlfriend and that we would be best friends, get along, and so on. Now, I get to rewrite the story I have about my son. In fact, he gets to write his own story, and I get to learn, witness, enjoy, and celebrate it.

The same way The Revolution caused realizations about what I didn't know about the world, Andrei coming out revealed to me the story I had made up about him. It revealed my expectations and limitations of what love looks like. This also busted up every other barrier in my mind. The borders of my heart opened up and I began to question and analyze every single detail of my life. Since then, every day has been a brand new day. Now, I walk with curiosity for discovering and learning about life, people, and myself.

I started to walk through my days and notice things that used to seem normal or didn't stand out. It was like my eyesight had adjusted like the lens of a camera adjusts to bring things into focus. I would look at the way something was and question it. "Why is it that way? Why do I believe it is that way? What other way might this be if I change my perspective?" Everything was falling apart in all the best ways. The upheaval, disturbance, and unrest of this Revolution was so healthy and I discovered even more of the world. My perception started expanding on a whole new level!

I will share much more toward the end of this book, but Andrei's coming out thrust me into more thoughtful conversations in the LGBTQ world. I found myself on stages and seminars as an advocate for gender identity reform and normalization. I could identify with the people I found myself surrounded by and this became a major part of my career and success. This was such an out-of-body experience which I will explain much more about in part four.

What I want to share now is the coming out I had to do following our conversation and his heart-wrenching question: "Mom, have you had to ever come out as straight?"

I had not. I was a straight, white woman. This came with its own obstacles, but coming out was not one of them. Most people were able to assume correctly about me and I never once had to explain, justify, or defend my heterosexuality. I was suddenly amazed by this fact and troubled by the way this was all set up.

I had never had to come out for myself, but I will tell you something that grew me throughout this situation was coming out as having a gay son to family and friends. There was a shift that happened almost immediately. When my child came 'out of the closet,' the next minute, I felt 'in the closet.' A stream of questions began flowing through my head, "Who do I tell? What should I tell? How can I be honest and protect my child's privacy?" The questions rolled right through, one after another. This was an interesting experience and I recognized feelings of hesitation and shame that would creep in. I love my son and I am so proud of him. This made me willing to fully experience this part of the process. Those embarrassing feelings were not mine. They were me bracing for the impact of other people's opinions of my son or my parenting.

It was so interesting and educational to walk through it all. To witness myself telling others that my son is gay taught me more about the boundaries, standards, and expectations I perceive from others. This Revolution launched me into yet another layer of the depths of my own soul-searching journey. This was the kind of search that leads you to find things you cannot unsee, admit things you can't unsay, and discover things you can no longer hide. I could no longer hide behind blissfully ignorant, blind, or distracted.

Questioning every construct started to put holes in my reality. Things I once considered as fact or truth fell apart under a microscope. In the midst of this exploration, ending the marriage with Dean blew the doors right off of the transformation that was already in process. I had been gently poking around and investigating sexual orientation and gender identity. Little did I know, this would send me spiraling down the rabbit hole of my own identity.

After a few years in New Zealand, Dean and I began to struggle. I wanted more from him and he wanted more space. This felt like a communication issue and I figured if my son could come out as gay, Dean could share what he was struggling with. This became a constant battle. We tried therapies, coaches, and counselors, but the harder we held on, the more we strangled what we had.

The end of my relationship with Dean unexpectedly accelerated my soul search. A couple of years prior, Andrei's coming out set something in motion. My third divorce strapped me to a rocket ship of transformation that blasted off into oblivion. This oblivion included exploring my past lives, my current life, and my future. It was like my little bit of curiosity about what could be different was thrust into overdrive to show me exactly how different things could be. My life began changing drastically at a very rapid rate.

My search into my past uprooted, buried, and repressed memories that shocked me. As if a dam had burst, once the floodgates opened, there was no closing them. There was no unseeing and unhearing what had revealed itself. There was just accepting, handling, and releasing it all.

The upcoming portion of this book is centered around forgiveness. It is about the phase of my life that served as the portal through which my soul level freedom was granted. Andrei's coming out shifted an integral part of me that served as the rock that started the avalanche of discovery, release, and evolution. This was completely uncomfortable and totally worth it.

Throughout this portion of the book, I will discuss the phase of life in which I went into the depths of my being to find peace. I will be sharing some of my darkest discoveries that birthed a new, lighter me.

This was the part of my story that I didn't want anyone to know about, and yet, it was so clear that this was the part of my history that needed to be told. This portion of my life was what truly made this book possible, because before this level of my transformation, the book was being written within me. Because of this phase, I became the woman who *could* write this book.

Before I was ever ready to write a book, this poem came out of me. Titled *Past. Present. Future.*

Past. Present. Future

My Past stopped by, one night
And got me so upset
Wanting to bring to light
The reason why I left.

It sneaked inside my mind
Start playing with my thoughts
The Present wasn't blind
Told Past to get lost.

Listen you ugly Past
You are in the wrong room
Already swept your mess
And thrown away the broom

It's clean in here now
I disinfect all over
So help yourself out
You can stay no longer.

I'm open just for Future
It is my new best friend
It makes me rich and richer
Day by day, to the end

This piece portrays my experience of transformation and the way it commands you and demands of you. The ride of transformation is one that will take you places you never thought to go, but it will also take you further than you ever dreamt you could get. Transformation is a continuous death and rebirth process that makes a new life available, even when it wasn't a new life that you were going for.

It is through The Revolution that the revelations become available. The border that opened up in Romania opened up my mind. The borders that opened up with Andrei's coming out opened up my heart. The borders that opened up in transformation, opened up my life. It hasn't always been easy but it's always been worth it. Allow me to show you how true freedom and liberation of the soul is possible. Follow me.

Chapter 13

Unraveling

What I have learned about those phases of growth we spin through in life - those lesson spirals - is that we walk out of the back end of it different than when we walked in. No matter how fast we trip from one to the next, we have grown through each one. This was noticeably true for my marriages.

My first marriage with Sorin was young, true love. Our fourteen years together were fun, happy, and exciting, but the divorce had me question what was actually real in all those years together. He left me, and although I learned after our divorce that I was better off without him, that didn't make it any easier. Knowing that after the fact didn't prevent the pain of heartbreak and failure in the moment. I knew I deserved more and to be treated with respect, yet it still took a lot of courage to let go. The abruptness of our split charged the breakup with hatred and rage.

My second marriage had a much different focus: survival. My relationship with Fred was a long experience of fearing for my life. I was constantly in fight or flight mode. The trauma of living with constant dread does a number on your central nervous system. I was always tense and watchful.

I will never forget the feeling that overtook my body the one and only time Fred came close to hitting me. I was so scared for my life that I grabbed a knife, jumped on the couch, and threatened that if he *ever* touched me that I would kill him in his sleep. Holding that knife in my hand, I was launched into my very own nightmare, "Holy shit! I am just like the people from back in my country, going for the kill with their knives." I couldn't believe who I had become at that moment. I was more scared of what I was able to say and possibly do, than I was scared of what was making me have that kind of response. I felt a certain kind of gross inside, but that didn't matter in this exact moment. This was life or death to me.

The primal attack mode I was in must have made my message clear, because he never did hit me. I was half his size so jumping on the couch was my best attempt to seem scary and serious, but I was frozen inside. I was grateful my message was received but I definitely had no idea if it would work. I was just completely out of all other options in that marriage.

Both relationships were two very different spirals and both took me upward. I made my way through two very different life experiences in each. When I think back to the entirety of my life, I am amazed at how many loops I have made it out of alive. I am forever grateful. There are some that I really wasn't sure if I would ever get out of.

After two divorces, you can guess that inner critic was playing games with my self-worth. I felt like shit, and used. Where I come from, if you are a divorced, single mom in her thirties, you are old, you are garbage, and nobody will want you. This was a common sentiment. Men went for young women who might be considered untouched. This cultural norm has caused so much damage, not just for myself, but for countless others.

I've been told and convinced that "Nobody will ever want a divorced woman with a child, and for sure, there is something wrong with her if her husband left." I was also an embarrassment for my family. I was the first one to bring this shame upon my parents and none of my family has ever let me forget that.

Two divorces really messed with my identity. My Romanian inner critic voice had a lot to say about being a worthless piece of shit and I totally believed her. I began to unravel, or at least my worth did. I hated myself so much and hated that I was in this situation. Finding myself and my power was next to impossible during my time in the shelter, when everyone was trying to encourage me to love myself. Everything seemed to be falling apart, and so was I.

As I have shared about my journey, the story goes: I got on my feet, I got the job, I started to heal, I found self- love, and I found love with another again. A real fairytale, I tell ya. All joking aside, so much of my relationship with Dean has been storybook like. He came around when I had finally felt fine on my own and still managed to sweep me off my feet.

When it came to the unraveling of this relationship, it felt like exactly that; a slow falling apart. With the previous two marriages, it was all drama. There was loud fighting, screaming, and fierce protecting. My relationship with Dean just seemed to be continuously slipping through my tightly gripped fingertips. I could never really secure my grasp at the end and it caused much more sadness than anger.

It was my heart that experienced this particular break-up. In the previous two, I had to use my head. It was what I knew best; shut up your heart and use your brain. I relied on logic, reason, and planning to process my first two divorces, but no previous strategy seemed applicable to this separation. I couldn't use my work ethic to figure this one out. I had to feel my way through it and this caused the intense transformation that I referred to in the previous chapter. This break-up launched me into the deep, internal work that I had previously never explored. The way I recognized this lesson loop to be different was that it was time for me to learn how to have a healthy break-up, and so, that is what I attempted to do. While I still didn't fully learn how to live with a man, I was ready to learn how to break up with a man and give myself space and time to heal.

There were so many times that we tried to work it out. We went back and forth, *over and over*. So many aspects of our relationship worked, but we had to work on the little things and it was the little things that pulled us apart. The love was there, the communication and full commitment was not. We were in that back-and-forth process while I was at a seminar in San Diego when I had the realization "I am losing control of my life." This tugged on my heartstrings and unraveled my power and self-worth, again. I recognized this feeling and knew I needed to start accepting what was happening. This was previously unrecognizable to me because I had always used anger to fuel my breakups. This empowered me to walk away without looking back. Without the anger, I was constantly tempted not just to look back but to go back. This was harmful to both our hearts. There was so much pain wrapped up in the process of letting go.

When we were breaking up I decided that I needed to start getting into the headspace that Dean had died. This may seem a bit dramatic and even morbid, I know, but it was the only way I could reframe this break-up to make sense to me. People don't die to hurt you. They just die, we get to miss them, love them, and celebrate our time together. This helped me comprehend our break-up without losing my worth. I had to let myself believe and accept that this had nothing to do with our ability to love and be loved.

Without cutting him off in rage, it was the only way that I could cope with things ending after he had messaged me "I'm done" while I was at the retreat. It felt real. I was tired. Without anger, I had no fight in me, just this deep sense of grief. It was the first time I accepted what he said and took off my wedding ring. I could feel myself letting it be so. It would be ideal to say, "I took off my wedding ring and a weight was lifted off my shoulders." It wasn't. I took off my wedding ring and a new weight pressed down on my chest. I couldn't breathe.

I was in a whirlwind of manifestations and emotions. Still at the retreat, I found out that my TEDx talk had been published. While I should have been excited about this, being a leader in the LGBTQ community made me a target for a lot of hate mail, angry words, and endless charged emotions and opinions from people. When I saw the congratulations email that my TEDx talk had been published, I was already upset about my break-up, and spiraled into overwhelming dread for what would be coming through my inbox over the next few days, weeks, and months.

People were coming up to congratulate me, and I was absent. I hid behind my non-existent excitement by saying that I was still processing, which I was, but it was more than that. What really held me back from celebrating was my marriage going down. What should have been one of the peak moments of my career turned into a nightmare that made my stomach *churn*.

Upon returning from the retreat, we *still* did our best to make it work. Something that confused me was how people could love each other so much and also not be compatible for each other. I came to the conclusion that I have never really seen healthy love displayed in my life and so when we had something even half good, it seemed out of this world. I don't think either of us really wanted to give that up, but that just meant that we weren't facing the fundamental facts. We had done our best and we weren't a good fit for what we were each creating individually. Some of the differences that we could have previously overlooked became too obvious to ignore. I actually found this to be positive, because I knew that we both contributed to each other's growth. We just so happened to grow in different directions and at a different pace. The difference was that now, I could be with that truth peacefully.

Through all the back-and-forth of trying to make it work, I scheduled a trip to Bali. Two days before my plane left, the coronavirus pandemic caused it to be cancelled. I was upset. I just wanted to go far away from all of the mess. While both of us wanted to leave the house, the opposite happened. The coronavirus pandemic sent both of us and Andrei to work/ school from home. With everyone at the house, I started to feel crowded and stuck.

Being home together had us considering working it out, and in yet another attempt to fix it, we would have dinners together. Except one night, our dinner was different. Dean cooked the meal, set the table, and while we sat there, said for the final time, "I want out." I immediately lost my appetite.

This absolutely enraged me. Dean's strategy hurt more than he probably planned because he tore open an old wound from my first husband breaking up with me over coffee, and now this time, over dinner. I was so simultaneously defeated, hurt, and angry that now I was the one who was done. I knew that I couldn't go through another "left behind" experience. Right there, in that conversation, with all the hurt and tears, we came to the first agreement in a long time: I was the one that got to leave. I was going to move back to America.

Although I was angry and ready to go, it didn't stop my heart from breaking. It didn't seem to stop the pain. That night, I went into Andrei's room to cry. After everything we had been through together, I trusted him with my life. To this day, I am not afraid to let Andrei see me emotional, hurt, and messy, and he is reliably able to be with me in my times of need.

From as far back as our time in the women's shelter, my son was an incredibly perceptive child. I remember when the shelter volunteers surrounded me and interviewed me. They wouldn't leave me alone, and I told them it was my child who needed the attention and care. I will never forget when one of the volunteers brought him in to ask him why we were at the shelter and his response was so simple:

"Fred is nice to us when other people are around and he is mean when they are not. He tells my mom he loves her, but then he makes her cry. That's not how you love someone, so we left." That's it. I was dumbfounded at how easily he understood. He understood that, as a six-year-old, and he imparted that same practical knowledge to me when I went to him after Dean and I officially split. Being so calm and rational, he simply said, "mom, you knew this was inevitable. It hasn't been working out for a while."

I knew it. It didn't feel good. And I was *finally* willing to accept it. The unraveling of our relationship unraveled me in whole new ways, ways I didn't know were necessary. The end of this relationship was actually my greatest test because it tested the strength of my heart. Instead of relying on grit, strength, or smarts, I had to practice love, trust, and surrender. These were whole new realms I had never really worked in but the end of this relationship was the start of a new upward spiral, one that I essentially walked alone. You can bet there were plenty more Earth Angels to join me on the journey, but this phase was one I knew I had to take on solo if I was going to meet myself for who I really am.

Chapter 14

Letting Go

Through the help of others, I came to understand the phase of life I was going through as 'The Dark Night of the Soul.' Just another shitty spiral if you ask me, but I was glad someone offered me that perspective, because it was a deeper and darker time than anything I had ever faced. What is amazing is that the stories I have already told you about neglect, abuse, judgment, homelessness, and hardship do not compare to the phase of emotionally unpacking it all.

I went through those phases on a very physical level and the way that I survived them was by checking out mentally and emotionally. What happens to us when we do not acknowledge and process our traumas is that they stay stored in our bodies, physically and energetically. This is what happened to me, and I had to heal all the way back to my childhood. This was a heavy load to bear unknowingly and this felt intimidating to face at first.

I also knew I couldn't do this alone. This is when I enlisted help, beyond self-help books, from coaches, mentors, healers, energy workers, shamans, and more. For the last few years, I have intentionally put myself in the space of discovering and uncovering my hidden trauma. I willingly opened myself up to my mentors to receive guidance, support, and help with the healing process. As life continues, the lasting process of transformation occurs with each discovery, each release, each healing. The more we can heal, the deeper we can go. In reference to those upward lesson spirals, the sooner we can learn, the higher we can climb. Never earlier, never later.

When I got serious about doing this inner work, I hired the right team to guide me along the way. I also became aligned with new friends in this work who have supported me greatly at some of my weakest moments of processing, grieving, and healing.

I was so blessed to have an amazing relationship with Dean because at the age of seventeen, Andrei decided he wanted to finish school in New Zealand. Dean, although I am pretty sure he just liked my son more than me, was fine living together while Andrei completed high school. This unofficially made me an empty nester once I moved back to the States from New Zealand. This was another out-of-body experience to be on my own for the first time ever. Like, ever. No parents, no family, no husband, no son, no one. Me, myself, and of all my fabulous personalities.

I believe there are no mistakes in the divine timing of it all. Andrei coming out launched my curiosity. My break-up with Dean triggered my next level of transformation. All these co-creative components contributed to my healing, growth, and evolution. Once I had the room to figuratively 'stretch out,' all of these thoughts, feelings, and memories came flooding back. It was phenomenal to recognize how being surrounded physically was actually boxing me in energetically. With even just a few inches of breathing room, everything came rushing back.

I will share all that came rushing back in the next few chapters, but in this moment, I want to share an example of the rapid processing that can occur when the body is truly ready for transformation.

At one point, Dean asked me to attend a conference with him. This was pretty routine for us but I was feeling different this trip. I was feeling kind of 'picky.' The trip from Auckland to Roroura was about a two hour drive but instead of driving, I wanted to fly. It was only a forty-five minute flight and I did not want to be dealing with the motion sickness of driving on the windy roads.

In the morning of the conference, even though I really wanted to partic-ipate and see Dean's new talk, *something* wouldn't let me go. I simply let Dean know that I was going to stay behind. A bit confused, he asked if I was okay and I told him I was fine. By all accounts, I was fine. I just didn't really feel like going, so I didn't.

Something within me just wanted to stay behind and relax. We had breakfast together and when Dean left for the conference, I went back to the room and did nothing until two in the afternoon. When hunger hit me eventually, I went to the hotel's restaurant and ordered some food, but nothing tasted right. I even ordered more food but there was something off about it. I couldn't quite put my finger on this pickiness. Discomfort? Unsettled? Bored? Gas? I couldn't tell what was up with me so after a few bites of food, I gave up on eating and kept relaxing.

Later in the evening, out of nowhere, I had this immense pain in my gut. I was doubled over and ran to the bathroom. I will spare you all the gory details but you can imagine bodily fluids coming out of every exit point available. It was like a horror film. I only remember screaming, and I mean *screaming* at the top of my lungs in pain.

The pain was comparable to the pain of contraction. I was in labor pain with one constant contraction, no break, just this mysterious and continuous pain for about three hours. I tried to talk through it with Dean; he tried calling doctors, and doing everything he could. Finally, he called an ambulance, and I was rushed to emergency. Laying in the emergency room I wondered, "was it the flying and resting, a way to conserve my energy to prepare me for this pain?"

I had all a bunch of tests done but all my vitals were fine and I got the clearance to leave. It was midnight by the time I was free to go. We missed our dinner and I was starving so we ordered pizza when we got back to the room. While just sitting there eating my pizza, Dean looked over at me with the most freaked-out kind of expression. Not only was he concerned for my well-being, but he was also confused about not having a diagnosis. He is a scientist, he needed answers, but I didn't, not this time.

"Are you sure you are okay? I think you should get more tests done as soon as we get back," he said. "What if you have a tumor or something?"

"I'm fine." Somehow, I just knew I was. "What happened to me was beyond biology, Dean. If there were a tumor in me at this point, it would simply be another trauma manifesting and there's no medicine I want for that."

He wasn't thrilled with my answer but he didn't push me on it, either. What I hadn't taken the time to explain to him was that I knew I was approaching the end of a nine-year astrological cycle in my life and after this episode, it felt very clear to me that this was a rebirth of some sort. I *know* how 'woo-woo' that might sound but it is what I knew to be true and I didn't need an scientific explanation for it.

I knew that whatever happened to me that day was an energetic experience, not physical. To me, it occurred as an exorcism of all the pain stored over the last seven years coming out of me all at once as to vacate my body and leave me renewed and restored. I can't say that I was expecting it but after the odd day, the most out-of-the-blue pain I've ever experienced, and how healed I felt after, I was sure this wasn't a medical matter.

The next day we went to the best Polynesian Spa in the country. Being in the hot springs and receiving the couple's mud packing and scrub massage was exactly what I needed. We had been there before and loved it, but this time for me was different. I was more present, fully in my body, and peaceful. It felt ceremonial.

Those walks from one hot spring into the next hotter one was like a baptismal experience for me. I was being baptized from the rebirth of the previous day. With each dip in the water, each rinse took off another layer and cleansed the authentic self that was emerging. I could consciously sense becoming the new me. This brought me a level of peace I had never felt before.

I *did* agree to see my doctor when I got home. We did the tests and I was not surprised when everything came back negative and normal. I had no doubt this had been more of a spiritual and energetic experience than a physical one, because I could not ignore the series of events that followed. I allowed that 'new me' to show up in my life and work. I made brave decisions, broke some rules, and created my own. Most importantly, I raised my new voice. As a result, my career took off, my coaching business skyrocketed, I hit six figures, landed a TedX talk, won a $10k Challenge, and the list goes on. I smile about that day because I was so grateful to be relieved of all that pain stored in my body. I saw that my body needed to clear in order to soar without being held down or limited.

Everything was different from then on. I have been different from then on. There was a confidence born in me that day that still moves me forward, boldly. What I have come to understand about myself is that I am here to lead, share, coach, teach, and guide. I have clarity about being here on this Earth to question the way things are and test the norms. I'm known for asking provocative questions that inspire considering alternative perspectives.

Question what feels "right" for *you*, not the majority. That eventful extraction process in Rotorua took me through a portal of pain and transitioned me into who I was made to be.

From that point on, I have promised to be the me that was born that day. I am committed to going above and beyond the status quo and paving new pathways for humanity to practice unconditional love and acceptance. Letting go of all that stored pain and the identity that went with it freed me up to be the Simona Spark you know, and maybe even love.

I am here to champion people being themselves and having the freedom to be and to love in whatever capacity they want. As we move through this next chapter, I will share more about what I had to let go of in order to become all of who I was made to be. For the remainder of this book, we are going to be talking a lot more about who we were made to be.

We cannot raise our voice if we have nothing to say. Raising your voice is ineffective if you are speaking untruthfully or inauthentically. As we continue to move forward together, we will take a closer look at who we think we really are and what we came here to do. I will share more about how I learned to deliver my gifts with the world, and explain that we all have the same standing invitation. I invite you to be a contribution. We must flush out our own shitty trauma responses so that we can truly love each other into our wholeness. This is an opportunity to let go of anything that is holding you back or keeping you down so you can raise your voice and rise up to fulfill your purpose.

Chapter 15

Coming Out

The first time I ever talked with my sister about sex was my last year of high school. She came sprinting up to me on my walk home, panting "mom…found…a condom in the toilet," between breaths. She was doubled over with her hands on her knees, gasping for breath as she warned me. She had rushed over to find me to warn me about the wrath I was about to potentially walk into at home.

"Are you having sex?" she asked, still trying to catch her breath.

"Well, yeah. Are you!?!" I asked back.

"Yeah, but…that doesn't mean it's ours!" she said, finally being able to stand up straight and look me in the eye.

We weren't very close throughout our childhood, but we could sense the fear in each other in this moment. The fear of being caught was bigger than the shame, the embarrassment, or the discomfort of talking about sex. Not talking about it implied that we were having sex, but now the secret was out - at least between the two of us. Either of us would be in so much trouble if that condom were one of ours and we both knew it. Something we also knew is that our brother would never be in trouble if it were his.

It was so unfair and unequal that when my sister ran up to me with the news that there was a condom left in the toilet, we both knew to blame our brother. I didn't know if it was hers or not, but I didn't need to know. If it were mine, she wouldn't know either. We knew we would both face grave consequences, and my brother would get a pat on the back. No explanations could have saved us. It didn't matter that both of us were in exclusive relationships. I had been dating Sorin for two years already, and she had been, as an adult, in her relationship for four. That didn't matter at all. It was an easy decision.

As I have mentioned, in our traditional upbringing, men were free to be sexually active, or overactive, and women were expected to be well-behaved virgins. Especially during the teen years, the standard was that girls were to be behaved, should not date, and sex was prohibited until marraige. A girl being sexually active in adolescent years was shameful and punishable.

Boys, namely my brother, on the other hand, were permitted and even celebrated for being sexually active. There was just one requirement; don't get anyone pregnant. I remember hearing my mother talk about how he brought another girl home or how he was so popular with the girls, comparable to if he was getting good grades in school. It was like a sport or a skill. It made me shiver with disgust and frustration.

Finding a condom would be okay if it were her son's, but most definitely not her daughters', and thank God that mom was the one to have found it. If it had been my dad, we would have both been dead! She would call girls my brother would be with 'sluts' and 'whores.' She would make fun of them with one breath and brag about my brother and what he was doing with the next breath. She'd be proud of her son based on how pretty the girl was. It was unbelievable to me. The double standard was so obvious, ridiculous, and discouraging. This was not just our mom, either. This was, and still is, the story of so many other mothers holding double standards for their own children.

While passing the blame over to my brother made clear, logical sense, the fact that it was my last year in high school and I was having my first conversation about sex with my sister said a lot. Even back then, I knew this was weird. Just talking, or merely thinking about sex was shameful and unsafe for young girls. Despite the fact that I wasn't even a minor anymore, it was still taboo.

As an adult, when it came time to heal sexual trauma, I had to be able to talk about sex. I felt so much shame around the topic, and it made it difficult. It was not just shame about what I had experienced, but I saw how simply talking about sex, sexuality, sexual activity, harassment, abuse, and more caused fear and discomfort in me. What I came to realize was that in my childhood, I had been also violated mentally by the idea of a girl's sexuality being filthy, dirty, disgraceful, and more. I had been conditioned to believe that sexually active girls were trash and worthless. As a natural biproduct, I internalized that sex wasn't safe to talk about, and that it's not something to bring up. This prevented me, and I imagine so many young women, from getting help and support and living healthy lives.

This definitely limited me from asking for help when I was toward the end of finishing middle school. There was so much shame and loneliness in my experience of being sexually harassed by the city boys. Being seen as 'a stupid country girl' had more than negative academic consequences. I was seen as 'less than' and treated that way, too. Being harassed with inappropriate words, touches, and advancements was an everyday threat. This naturally put my body into a frequent emergency state of being. I was hardly ever able to relax.

I can vividly recall the details of a situation in middle school when someone came up from behind me in the street and put his hand between my legs. I remember the feeling, the wave of fear, that rushed over me when I felt a stranger's hand where it didn't belong. I can recall the laughter of others and how isolated and unsafe I felt. I can still hear the taunting and name-calling. I *still* felt like it was my fault. I was sure I must have done something wrong.

Worst of all, I remember the fact that there was no one around to protect me, stick up for me, save me, or comfort me. I had to attempt to defend and protect myself when I could hardly speak in that moment due to the shock and complete embarrassment. This was paralyzing in the moment and because I never shared about it, it continued to paralyze me for years to come.

Later in high school, walking home on a hot summer day, I was harassed by a man in his forties as I made my way past his house. He shouted sexual comments at me on the street, encouraged by two others, that brought me to tears. I didn't know what to do besides cry, run home, and believe it was my fault because too much of my body was exposed due to summer clothing.

When I got home, my dad was there with his brother. They caught me crying and asked me about what happened. They made me take them around the corner and show them which man made the comments. My uncle jumped on him and put his fist in the man's face and threatened him. This didn't make me feel safe, either. As much as I wanted that man to hurt the way he hurt me, this reactive act of violence didn't feel like the right answer. At the end of all that, I had been advised by my dad and my uncle to wear longer shorts. So it had been my fault, after all.

I felt frozen in fear every time a boy would make a comment or I could overhear people talking about me. The harassment continued through high school, and starting my relationship with Sorin felt like a safe haven. Adults allowing boys to think that it is okay to be sexual predators had a lasting negative ripple effect. It shaped so many of our societal behaviors and my own psyche.

It was a norm in our Romanian culture for boys and men to be aggressors, and it was reinforced by parents, teachers, and friends. Recognizing that being out after sundown would be dangerous because you could be raped was just terrible to me. Rape culture was a fact of life in the time that I grew up, and we didn't correct the behavior. The girls were expected to correct their behavior to fit that narrative. Not being out after dark was standard protocol and if you didn't honor that rule, you would be responsible for what happened to you.

In my adulthood, this definitely inspired me to raise my voice around the conversation of sex and sexuality. It has been a priority to me to normalize this conversation and create space for it in the world, because it is necessary. I suffered and struggled for so long because I felt like a couldn't talk about sex, which is common for many. There are just some people who aren't willing to hear about it or deal with it appropriately and it certainly discourages those who need help talking about it. We must make it known that just because some are unwilling to address the issue does not make this conversation good, bad, right, wrong, or divisive at all. It is just important. It can save lives. We must be willing to hold a conversation about sex and sexuality if we want to be free to live healthy lives.

I teach and preach this now with confidence, but this was not true for me even just a few months before committing to write this book. Being able to talk boldly about my sexual trauma has been a wound I have needed to heal and a skill that I have needed to develop. I want to share this because even as a successful leader and sexual health advocate, I can only explain this now because I have taken on the work for myself.

People have so many opinions about what gets to be shared and what doesn't. Sharing can be powerful and inspiring. Sharing becomes most powerful if and when that part of the story is healed, free of shame and blame. I want to be clear that this doesn't mean we don't have to wait to share our struggles *until* we are healed.

I want to encourage everyone to be responsible with who they share their trauma with and for what purpose. Healing is a delicate phase and sharing with trusted individuals is your healthiest option. There is a process of healing with each trauma where that story gets to be told from a place of victimhood, and eventually, from a place of understanding, acceptance, and love. Going to the right people at the right times will help with that process.

Even as I write this, that paralyzing fear is very present and real for me. It is making my fingers heavy and throat tight to think about raising my voice about some of the sexual trauma I have faced in my life. While I no longer need anyone's permission or approval of my own story, I'm still concerned about how this might be received. However, I am more committed to the impact of this story than how someone may perceive what they learn about me in this chapter. As I choose to share this story publicly for the first time, what is right over my shoulder, whispering in my ear, is all the judgment I have heard my entire life about girls being disgusting and shameful.

One thing that is important to me to clarify is that having grown up in that environment, I too adopted some of the judgments I had heard for so long. "How can she let something like that happen to her? How can she not remember? There's no way I would get myself into a situation like that." The internal dialogue goes on and on. In taking on the healing work, I have noticed how the judgments I was impacted by were ones that I kept and held onto to judge others with.

Call it a deflection, survival tactic, or whatever else you wish, I judged other women just like myself before I knew I was one of them. I didn't exactly realize what I was doing while I was doing it, because I didn't know I was a victim of sex trafficking when I was. In fact, I went on for twelve years before the visions and memories came flooding back into my consciousness.

You see, the human mind and body have this ability to 'forget' some of the most traumatic experiences in our lives. At the most functional level, this happens as to not thrust us into complete mental breakdown; to the point of no return from insanity. The mind will compartmentalize these memories so we cannot see them in our conscious mind, but that does not mean they don't exist or have gone away.

The trauma associated with all of these events has been existing in my body, even when my mind erased the event from my memory as a protective mechanism. The most painful and scary part of all is that trauma doesn't know time. No matter how old or how long ago the traumatizing event happened, when remembering that event, the pain feels as present as if it had happened today. Our body never forgets. Much like the saying, "God only gives you as much as you can handle," we are always equipped to handle what's been revealed to us in the process of healing and transformation.

As I shared in the previous chapter about the way in which my body exorcised all of my pain in one quick episode, the body stores these traumas in our energetic and physical bodies until they are identified and released. I believe that this is what can make people mentally and physically ill without much medical explanation. Storing low frequency traumas and emotions in the body can do long-term damage. The way to correct this and heal yourself is to identify and release what remains stagnant in the body.

I mentioned the divine timing of Andrei's coming out, my break-up with Dean, the growth of my business, and my own self-exploration. The memories that came up were stored within me for over a decade before my subconscious was able to unpack them. Do you think that I could have handled this memory a decade ago while homeless and lost? Hell no! First, I had to become someone who was strong enough to handle this discovery.

If I had had this recollection during my time in the shelter, I would have snapped. I imagine I would have ended up in the psychiatric ward because I didn't have the capacity to handle this information. If it came back to me during my immigration journey, I may not have been able to pass an interview to qualify for citizenship. Had these memories showed up while building a relationship or business, it all would have fallen apart, because that is exactly what happened to me when my memories of being sex trafficked resurfaced.

The first glimpse of this was revealed to me in 2019, when I was in North Hollywood planning my first in-person event in LA. It was a workshop for parents, and *get this*, the topic was sex and gender. When I was heading to the venue, I had this strange déjà vu experience. I felt slowed down by something, as if time itself had temporarily paused. I stopped with it and paused getting where I was going, and picked my eyes up to notice my surroundings. I explain this slowly but you wouldn't have noticed this experience if you were walking with me. It was only a brief moment.

"Huh," I thought. "This is where I worked when I was here for my three-month visa when I came to America for the first time." This amazed me. "And now I am hosting my first ever event on the same street. Life is so amazing." I was on the same street, I recognized the buildings, and I could see the luxurious apartment building where I had lived and worked for two months. Wow! Coincidence? It couldn't be.

I was having this internal dialogue of achievement and victory. Who would have ever thought that I'd be here eleven years later, while back then, leaving Romania was hardly even an option? I was feeling really proud of myself and my eleven-year journey of coming *full circle*. Definitely not a coincidence, a full circle. Without much more thought, I carried on with what I was doing and headed to the conference venue.

It wasn't for another year that I was prepared to see what my subconscious needed to show me. As I mentioned before, right after moving back to LA and living completely on my own, I went deeper into my healing. A month later, my body recognized that I had the time and space to process my own memories. I woke up one morning and clear memories came flooding through my mind. My breath got shallow and I began to panic as one image after another raced through my vision. I couldn't see out of my eyes. All I could see was the highlight reel rushing through my head. I also couldn't close my eyes to avoid what was revealing itself.

I fought. I kicked and denied and collapsed to the ground. It was torture, yet no one was doing anything to me in that moment. It was my mind showing me everything I never wanted to see. I couldn't accept it. I screamed and sobbed as I remembered. I cringed and cried as I watched the replay. I couldn't turn it off. I was spiraling, but this time downward, and fast. "Am I awake? This is a super vivid nightmare. Holy shit, I'm awake. These are my memories! My memories!"

I kept rubbing my eyes and burying my face in pillows as if I could suddenly make it go away, but it was my time to see. It was time to witness my own sexual trafficking abuse that happened to me back in 2008. I began to slow down my resisting and tried to focus on my breathing, but I just kept sobbing. I went on sobbing and feeling all that pain for days, but at some point, I accepted that I had to just allow it. I had to remember and I had to be able to be with it all. Being unplanned, I wasn't expecting what had gone on that morning, but I can at least say that I was prepared for it. It didn't make me any more willing in those first moments but as a woman doing the inner work, I was equipped for the situation.

In contrast to my childhood, I also had a community of support available to me to help me process what was happening in a healthy way. Talk about divine timing and Earth Angels - it was no coincidence that my friend Kenni was in my house visiting me from Texas for a few days when all this was revealing itself to me.

Kenni has always been the friend who is there by your side at just the right time. This woman is the woman who stepped into my life from out of nowhere, really. We knew each other through work and interacted here and there at some events, but we weren't really friends. When I qualified as an HCI $10k Challenge finalist and was supposed to fly to Dallas to give a talk in front of a thousand people, she called me to ask, "Does your family travel with you? Will anyone be with you at this event?"

"No," I said, "I know a lot of people at the event. I won't be alone, but nobody will be *with me*."

"Well," she said, "I was not planning to go to this event, but I'm coming, I won't have you be there alone," and just like that, she stepped in. As a finalist of the same challenge twice before me, she knew what that meant to me. This also meant she knew what to expect for this weekend. She did her job, making sure I was eating, resting, and saving me from the overwhelming number of people who wanted to talk with me. She would even tell me when to go to the bathroom. I had no idea what it took to be a speaker at such a big event. On top of all that, I won, so the rest of that weekend became way more overwhelming. Kenni helped me through all of it, with grace, kindness, and love.

As soon as I moved to LA, she planned her trip to visit me. Late one evening, while we were walking home from dinner, she stopped me and let this woman pass us. Once she was far enough, Kenni said that this woman was walking behind us at the same pace as us. She warned me, "we need to be aware that most sex trafficking victims are 'marked' by a woman."

"Marked?" I asked.

"Yes, women scout other women to be recruited or abducted as victims of sex trafficking. It is important you know that and keep a lookout," she informed me. I did not know this fact and it made the hair on the back of my neck stand up. I got the shivers, but we just kept walking.

Two days later I woke up to face the most hidden trauma of my life. Kenni stayed with me over the next few days to literally and figuratively hold me during my breakdown. Unlike my upbringing, I was allowed to speak up and share about what had happened to me. Kenni held the safe space I needed. She listened with compassion and loved me fully without judging, shaming, or correcting me. She was present and listened as I processed out loud and cried even louder.

The pain and embarrassment of these experiences made my whole body ache. I was falling apart, unraveling at every seam. There were days that I was so drained from the recalling, witnessing, processing, and releasing that I could hardly move. I lost my appetite and briefly, some self-love and self-worth.

As I've mentioned, I have previously judged women in my exact scenario, wondering "how could someone 'let' themselves be drugged?" or "how could someone not remember being sedated?" When I first came to California to work during my first visitor's visa, I remember working for a premier real estate agent. The job I remember doing was some kind of a housekeeper: anything from ironing clothes, picking up coffee, dropping off paperwork, and other routine tasks. I have few pictures from inside the apartment, but I don't remember the apartment. I do remember the hallways, the doorman, the amazing pool, and all the places that she took me surrounding LA. Previously, I never had memories or details about the inside of the apartment. Never, until now. All of a sudden, on that morning, I could see the rooms, the sheets, the faces. I was horrified.

I do not remember being drugged, sold, sexually abused, raped, and left there until the phone rang, "Want to see Santa Monica? Be downstairs in twenty!" I just remember that she took me everywhere. I still don't fully understand how I couldn't recognize that within my body but I know that the body can do miraculous things to survive. If I could consciously survive three hours of freezing weather the night Fred locked us out of the house, I can only imagine what I have survived in an unconscious state.

The greatest burden I remember feeling during these days of processing was the deepest sense of embarrassment and shame. I went over the pictures of her and places we visited together, over and over again. I never once felt hate toward her, but lots of self-judgments. I thought I was at my lowest in my relationship with Fred. Then, I felt at my lowest in the women's shelter, but in the days following this latest revelation, I felt at my absolute lowest. Lower than dirt. 'Scum of the Earth' kind of low.

"How could I let this happen? How could I not remember? How did I not know then? How?!?"

Old feelings of self-hatred made their way back. That small-Self, who I hadn't heard in a while teamed up with the inner bitch and they straight-up bullied me for a while. "You idiot. You piece of shit. You are such a disgrace. You are filthy. Go take a shower you filthy, piece of shit."

Every cell in my body was aching and I was being wrung out. I cried my eyes dry. I screamed my voice away. I exorcised every ounce of energy in me that existed in those memories. By the week's end, I felt as used as I believed myself to be. I was sedated by my own shame and misery.

Digesting these memories required every bit of growth, knowledge, and awareness I had ever collected over the years. The pain was immense but every breakdown leads to a breakthrough. It took months, and honestly, I think that I will always be working on healing this wound, but I have begun to regain my sense of self over time. By committing and recommitting to a greater life, I have been able to restore my sense of self and worth.

As you might be able to imagine, this process only made me stronger. For years prior, I had been coaching, speaking, and leading in an industry of self-development, acceptance, and evolution. I had all the tools and foundation to handle this. However, it was equally a test of those tools and the strength of that foundation.

This experience also opened up a new avenue of transformation for me. With all of this trauma previously stored in my body now released, there was new space available in my being to do this work on a deeper level. I became even more serious about cleaning up my energy. This led me further down the path of self-exploration and healing. Doing this work with and for others has empowered me and provided me clarity about who I get to be in the world. I remembered that this was the work I promised myself I would do so many years before.

Me first

I'm happy, but still feel sad
I'm angry but I'm not mad
I'm not alone, yet feel so lonely
Nobody can fix this. Me only

I don't know what to do
How to face the real truth
Decisions I must take
The right ones, for my future's sake

I know deep deep inside of me
There is the answer I can't see
What should I do to bring it out
What should I do to hear it loud

They say that no matter what
I should fight for what I want
And I should choose the best for me
No matter what that it will be.

Is it that simple? I'm not sure
Is not just me in this world
The choice I make for myself
Will bring to others some effect

I didn't thought will be so hard
To speak my mind and to stand up
For what I want and what I need
For my own life and my beliefs

Even is hard, is really worth it
To make a life I always wanted
With my own hands and working hard
So I can look back and be proud

It is that simple, works like this!
I can't have everybody pleased
Some will be happy, some will be sad
I need to take care of myself!

Once I gained my footing back, I recruited myself to take care of myself, and began again with the healing work. I chose to actively look inward. I chose to go in for the memories and dig them all out. I want to share with you that when we become willing to look, what we need to see will be shown. I was shown those memories because I had become willing to look. I started exploring sexuality and relationships and success. I had become curious about everything, and in turn, everything revealed itself.

This experience has taught me that I can be with anything and everything that comes my way and I can support others in processing, releasing, and receiving. Coming out of my own closet meant letting things come out of me. Arriving to a point at which I can share the full truth about my life has come only after being willing to face it for myself. The work it took on my end was learning how to be able to shift into understanding, acceptance, grace, and forgiveness.

I have claimed to be a leader and this work has held me to my word. It has shaped and refined the leader that I know myself to be. I have shared how the creation of this book has been a forty-four year journey. Everything that has ever happened *to me, with me, at me*; everything was *for me*, regardless if it felt like that or not. Every step contributes to the whole picture, every step matters. The experience of remembering my sex trafficking is what made it clear to me that I must raise my voice even higher to encourage others to raise their hands for support.

We are not alone on this journey. Your small Self would love for you to think that so that you never become big; so that you never get help. We can overcome any obstacle and face any barrier to a thriving life by being willing to be vulnerable and ask for help. If you become willing to raise your voice, you show the force that fuels all things that you are also willing to have your best self come forth. Come out. Speak up and share who you are so that you may live your fullest life.

Be brave enough to **stand up** and **speak up** about your truth. **Show up** and share who you are. Live your fullest life and **step up** to each experience.

Chapter 16

Raising My Vibe

Raising my voice has taken forty-four years to master. Raising my vibe is something I have come to understand in more recent years. I never believed in all that woo-woo, hippy shit about manifestation, vibration, and meditation when I started out. Then, without calling it any of that, I saw the same results materializing in front of my eyes.

This began to happen more and more, and the better I felt, the more results I was producing. The act of raising my vibe was occurring and I still wasn't calling it that. I knew what I was doing involved hard work, resilience, grit, and strength, but something started to shift.

Being successful kept getting easier and easier over time and I noticed that I didn't have to work as hard to produce my desired results. There seemed to be a lot of natural flow and a lot of synchronicities that I knew couldn't have come from forcing things to happen. Things were just happening perfectly.

Instead of 'making' things happen, I started watching things happen. This was a phenomenal experience and it started to create new patterns of thought, too. I began to explore new concepts, such as manifestation. I opened my heart back up to spirituality and felt a new sense of support present in my life. All of these tiny and subtle components were becoming obvious contributing factors to my vibe rising and thus, the elevation of the quality of my life.

My life was going pretty well when I ended up in a hot air balloon in Egypt to celebrate Dean's birthday. I had never been in a hot air balloon and noticed how many new things I was doing on a weekly and monthly basis now. Both the quality and direction of my life were heading upward, just like this balloon we had entered.

I had never been in a hot air balloon, so I was surprised when the operator fired up the blast furnace and we didn't go skyrocketing into the air. I don't know why I thought that we were about to move quickly, an inexplicable expectation that made my heart pound. Instead, it was quite the opposite; we made this very slow ascension into the sky, and with that, my heart started beating at a peaceful pace. What I hadn't really understood about hot air balloons is that once filled, they would be ready to float, but the sandbags keep them on the ground.

Almost immediately, I had this rush of a new realization. With each drop of each sandbag, I saw my life flash before my eyes. Bag number one, my childhood. Bag two, my first divorce. Number three, Romania. Four, Fred. Bag number five, citizenship...at this point, I don't remember how many bags were attached to that basket. I just remember the weightlessness I felt as each sandbag of my life officially fell away from me. While holding Dean's hand and sharing the basket with other people, I was having my own experience, as if I was alone in there.

My shoulders dropped back and my heart opened up wide as I took a deep breath in. I was brought back to my reality as the operator sent a breath of loud fire into the balloon, lifting us higher and higher. I was happy to be back where I was because I took a moment to look over the side of the basket.

From where we floated, I could see the edges of Egypt. We flew above Luxor, above the Nile River, and above the Valley of the Kings. From our elevation, I could see for miles and miles. I noticed that there were people down there, on the ground, living their day-to-day lives, and that this perspective would always be available. I realized that I had lived most of my life from the ground-level perspective, and that if I had had access to this view, I might have been able to see better things ahead. Day-to-day life might not have seemed so scary, if I had known more of what was coming.

I finally came to understand what raising my vibe meant. I could feel it vibrating in my bones. I had butterflies in my stomach and I was as eager to get back to Earth, despite being so happy to be in that balloon. I knew that I had developed into a woman who could create her amazing life with ease, grace, flow, and a calm power of knowing my identity. This experience was just a few days after my awakening in the Grand Pyramid. Even though flying in the hot air balloon was something we were doing to celebrate Dean's birthday, for a few sacred moments, I drifted away from the reason we were there. I drifted into my body to notice the calm and peace matching the calm, slow movement of the balloon.

It has been through constantly owning and raising my voice that I have been empowered to get to a level of hot air balloon status. I was floating through life knowing that I had everything I needed to create a life that I love.

We all have this power within us constantly. The difference in the lives we all experience is based on how tapped in we are to that infinite power. The results we produce are reliant upon how faithfully we own ourselves and our gifts, because it is the ownership that grants us the access to soar above any and all obstacles on our way to greatness.

Resistance creates friction. Friction creates dysfunction. It has been through the depth of work in the area of acceptance and forgiveness that I have been able to release all resistance to allow the love of others, a higher force, and myself to flow freely. It is that flow that has allowed me to float. It is that freedom that has liberated me from all limitations.

The essence of freedom can only be experienced by those willing to soar.

Paper Never Forgets!

Write down your insights.

Part 4

Raising My Voice

Chapter 17

Coming Home

Coming out as a victim of sex trafficking has set me free in more ways than one. A voice has been given to that part of me and when I started to listen, I learned she had a lot to say. I learned a lot about myself and my needs when I took the time to pay attention to her. Learning to let her speak was like learning to speak up for myself all my life. It took courage and a willingness to take a step out of my own comfort zone. At different stages of my life, the scary stages and consequences were different but the lesson and skills were the same: stand up and speak up to get your way.

I don't mean "my way" in some entitled sense. It means what's best for me. It means having the courage to break the rules made by others, and doing the inner work to identify my own rules. It also represents not compromising my best interests for the desires of others, which means upgrading my personal boundaries. This has made the most powerful difference in my life. Taking a stand for 'getting my way' moved me through and beyond relationships and circumstances that cost me my health, wealth, sanity, and freedom.

This is so important because if we are limited, then we are not delivering our gifts. If we are surviving, then we are not thriving. I lived from a place of surviving for far too many years, and still to this day, there are some leftover reactions from that place. This is what causes hurt and harm in the world. It's not our struggling and suffering that prevents us from ever entering a conversation about what's possible. It is the shame and blame attached to our experience, the lack of healing of that experience, that stops us. This stops us from being whole, healed people, just living our whole, healed lives in the world.

For example, Andrei's willingness to come out as gay ended his internal suffering. With permission to be open, to share, and to express himself, he freed himself from the turmoil of considering what to do, what to say, and how to be. By communicating his truth, he now made it to the next level of being himself and exploring that truth. Exploration leads to development and development leads to mastery. Even if it takes years to master ourselves, the willingness to accept, express, and explore grants us access to our fullest lives. When we show up for our lives, we have the opportunity to step up with each experience. This is how we spiral up to grow and evolve.

His willingness to explore activated mine. I told you, he is my teacher. I was ready for the next level, a deeper exploration than I've done before. When I began to question things, I became free from the way things were, or at least the way I believed them to be. Because I opened up my mind and heart, I had room for more and new truths. Clearing what I believed to be true made space for the repressed truths to come up and out. I'm no longer afraid to ask provocative questions. In fact, that is my norm now. Curiosity and willingness to learn new perspectives are the gateways to expansion. We simply can't find new answers if we don't ask new questions.

The outdated and deeply imprinted limiting beliefs surfaced and I let those go, too. This was such an expansive time of my life. Expanding my capacity to be with all of the parts of me helped me shift into the woman who can be all of who she is. Coming out as the whole me helped me step into a whole life. This process introduced me to myself.

Coming out enabled me to come home. All my life, I had been running, moving, wandering, and chasing. Shedding layer after layer and spiraling through loop after loop brought me full circle back to myself. It led me home to my heart, and now, I create my life from a true and authentic place.

We are always doing our best to do this. So, next time you hear yourself saying "I should have done it better," remember that you couldn't have. It's not as if you had a better option available and you chose the lesser one. You did the best you could have at that moment. We *are* trying to have our best lives, even if that means we make a few mistakes or wrong turns along the way. Those are the lesson spirals that evolve us upward *through* a loop of experience.

We don't always have the tools available to us to create what we can see in our minds. It can get frustrating to be able to dream clearly and not see what is holding us back. It is by going inward that we can identify our unique blocks and barriers that stop us. Once seen, they can be dismantled. When we are willing to look, we will be shown, and we will also be provided the people, places, and opportunities to cause the breakthroughs that will lead us home.

Coming home to my LA, top floor apartment after revisiting Andrei in New Zealand was very different than arriving on that first day. There was no echo. It was a fully furnished home with artwork hung on the walls. Warm and filled with my essence, it also had a fridge filled with food and fresh flowers on the table upon my arrival. My friend, Cassandra, oversees Spark Penthouse while I travel and she is one of my chosen sisters; the best friends I could ever ask for.

I met Cassandra four years ago through a request post in our coaching group. We both needed roommates for a travel weekend in our program. She said yes, we changed phone numbers, and we met for the first time at the door of our rental. She was just moving from Florida to Connecticut, I had just moved from Minnesota to New Zealand, and here we were, at the same coaching event, and now weekend roommates in Dallas, Texas.

We quickly became best friends. We set weekly zoom calls and for the past four years, we have kept those calls; supporting each other, witnessing each other's journey, and being there for each other no matter where we were in the world. Little did we know that we would both end up living in Los Angeles in the same neighborhood years later. Life happens like that and I love it.

Now, we get together for girls' night and get excited about how great our lives are. I still sit back in amazement even when we're just sitting around, laughing over non-alcoholic champagne. I think about how amazing it is to be sitting on a top floor apartment in LA while Andrei has his own life and I am back on my own.

A huge portion of my life has been spent surviving. Back when I was writing down my future on flashcards, I could envision what my life would look like, but now, I get to experience it firsthand. I can feel the sense of fullness, joy, liberation, and peace that comes from being 'home' in my body. There is no more escaping myself or my circumstances. Settling into who we know ourselves to be without a need to fix or figure out allows us to be present and grounded in who we are. Being energetically satisfied brings us to a resting place that allows us to be where we are in each moment. As we move through the rest of this book, we are going to look at the power of claiming who you really are.

Take a look at your life and notice where you are still chasing, and trying to prove or win something. This is distracting you from the amazing life that is already available in every moment. So many people never even arrive at a place of fulfillment in a way that they can find their body and mind at rest and decide what it is that they want to do next.

When we slow down to explore life instead of speeding to a destination, we stop tripping through lesson loops one after the other. In fact, we stop needing to enter them in the first place. Imagine that from a whole, complete, and healed place, you would be able to live a life in which you are simply applying and teaching the lessons. This is a completely different experience of life.

This is where the joy of living gets sparked. When all our needs are met, we know how to get new ones met, because yes, you are a human who will continue to have needs. When our basic needs of safety and shelter are met, we can pick our eyes up off the ground. We can stop walking simply to avoid landmines and lift our gaze onto the horizon. With our shoulders back and chins up, we no longer operate from a survival mindset, we promote the thriving mindset to take the lead. We can have far more fun, witness more blessings, and step into opportunities as they present themselves. As we spiral up to a new level, more is revealed to us, and we can see further. It works much like climbing a mountain; the higher you get, the wider the horizon becomes.

We will shed light on what's possible when we are energetically home. This "home" is when we are most filled with the spirit of life force energy that inspires creative action. This is when we start passion projects, movements, missions, foundations, and more. Coming home to your body and truth makes you glow in a way that catches the attention of others as well.

There will always be a wide spectrum of feedback when you are in your freedom flow but the lower vibe criticisms, from others or straight from your head, won't have the same impact anymore. I often say that people no longer can hurt my feelings. There are times when criticism can still hurt a little, but there is nothing anyone can say to make me stop going for my dreams. This chatter certainly won't stop you from doing what you know to do and being who you know to be. It is up to you to keep pursuing your dreams regardless.

As we proceed through this next part, I will share my experience of fully accepting the gift that I am and the gifts that I have. Understanding that accepting your greatness is not arrogant but actually your duty. It is what will transform you into a contributing member of society. Think about it; if a carpenter never accepted his gifts, who would build our homes? How about a mechanic? Lord knows, we need them to accept their gifts. What about doctors and lawyers and accountants? And can we get a hand for the technology gurus? Let's please get an amen and a hallelujah for the folks who have answered the call of loving logistics because I have no idea where I would be without their greatness and contribution.

So, if we take a look at how logical it seems that their accepting your gifts helps others, what stops you? If a leader avoided his leadership, who would cause change and organization in the world? If a healer hid behind her fear, who would guide us home? If a chef never let himself express his love of food, my son wouldn't be inspired to cook elaborate meals.

I will be sharing the joy of sharing your gifts and inviting you to seriously consider what they are. One provocative question I have for those who look for their calling and purpose is, what if we all have a common pur-pose? What if we all have the same duty to find ourselves, to come out as who we are, and allow our unique gifts to open our unique pathways to our unique dreams?

Beyond that, consider what it looks like to apply those gifts to a craft, business, relationship, or project. Now, before we get too far off track, I want to share how this isn't about starting the next trendy thing or inventing something. This invitation is about following what sets your soul on fire, it's about giving more energy to the things that excite you and standing up for what you believe in. How this manifests can look seven and a half billion different ways. What is truly important is that you look and decide for yourself. The most important work I have ever done in life was finding myself.

Finding myself

Mirror, mirror on the wall
You're able to show my soul
Looking in my mirror
I don't see anybody
What's wrong with my mirror?
It shows me just a body

I just can't remember
Where I lost myself
I do have to find *me*
Starting with my past.

I'm looking through the *strengths*,
I don't see me there;
Then turn to *confidence*,
I'm not anywhere.

Keep searching through *emotions*
Looking through *happiness*
Try to not lose my patience
I have to find me! Yes!

I turn to *all my dreams*
And look through *all I love*,
Searching through *my beliefs*
And also, through *my goals*.

I just don't remember
Where I lost myself;
I do have to find me,
I'm done searching in my past.

Start looking in the present,
I do see some of me;
Digging through my feelings,
I find reality:

I always have been here,
I never lost myself
Just didn't really hear
What *my inside voice* said.

I see now clear *all dreams*,
Confidence, strengths, and *beliefs*
All emotions, all I love,
Happiness and *all my goals!*

Mirror, mirror on the wall,

You're able to show my soul.

Looking in my mirror,

Everything's so bright,

I can see my future,

Build it strong and right!

I have had the most fun in life by following my heart. My voice and vibe rise together now as I walk in my purpose and with my authentic identity. Being fully me is a winning situation because everyone around gets the best me who is present, kind, compassionate, honest, and fiercely loving. Around me, people can count on getting the truth and the guidance to get where they're going and how to get there fast. Buckle up, my friend. We're going to take a wild ride.

Chapter 18

From Captive to Captivating

Going from an immigrant with no English to a TEDx stage for my first talk ever has surely been a wild ride. There are days that I am amazed by my own story and series of life events. To transform my situation from codependent and reliant to generous and interdependent, is a transformation that was worth writing a book about.

While I purposely wrote a memoir instead of a workbook, sharing my story with you has served many purposes. I set out to share proof and inspiration that anyone can get where they see themselves going. It is safe to take risks and follow your dreams. I want immigrants and native citizens alike to know that the resources to succeed are always available if you are willing to raise your voice. I didn't write a workbook because my intention is not to have you follow my voice. I want you to find, listen to, and follow your own.

Although I was highly successful in Romania as a consultant in sales, insurance, and banking, my smarts and humor for that matter, did not translate into English. I have a robust Romanian vocabulary, and felt insecure when I first got to America. Coming here and not being able to communicate and connect caused me to lose my sense of belonging and confidence. Instead of being able to use my intelligence and skill, I was forced to rely on my hard work. This effectively turned me into a part-time employee working for minimum wage when I was finally able to work in the states.

Something that surprised me was realizing that communicating in English would take away my spark. You guys, I am *so* funny, at least in Romania. Without an understanding of slang and advanced word choices, coming to a new country removed my ability to joke and have fun with the people around me. I would always get feedback from Americans about how rude, mean, blunt, and harsh I was, but in reality, I just didn't know how to crack a joke.

It makes me smile to this day the way Tammie at the optometrist's office would laugh at how bad my humor was. She was funny, and one of the few who encouraged me to keep trying. It wasn't the jokes I made or even how terrible the translation of the joke I made was, no one found me very funny, except for me, anyway. If you hear some of the European to English translations, they are funnier than some of the jokes most Americans tell. I am mostly teasing, but I am not kidding about how much this put a damper on my true personality and ability to connect, which killed my spirit.

Without the ability to be my charismatic self, I was again forced to rely on my work ethic. This kept me as an employee of others for longer than I would have liked. At the deepest level, I am an entrepreneur at heart. Back in Romania, I was trained as an entrepreneur—always working with a contract and for commission instead of being an employee with a fixed or guaranteed paycheck. I love to pave paths for myself and with others to give everyone the opportunity to get paid to be themselves.

Something I believe about leadership is that we are all leaders in our own right. This goes back to the last chapter when I mentioned that sharing your gifts can manifest in seven and half billion ways. How we share the gift that we are is as important as understanding and accepting the gift that we are. This aspect of the conversation is about vibe. If we all vibrate at the frequency of being a gift and contribution to this world then we naturally will be.

This is very different than vibrating at the frequency of broken, hurt, angry, resentful, or worthless. To be able to identify our value and make it part of our identity is a contribution to humanity. To be one less person sucking up the energy of others or constantly needing help. If you are feeling like you are attracting people that drain you, you could start with the question "what frequency am I vibrating at?" and face the reasons you have attracted this type of person in your life.

You know the saying 'opposites attract' right? Screw that! We are not magnets. We are human, and we are attracted to people who live at the same vibration. There is no coincidence about who we meet and for how long we walk the path of life together. While this is a complex phenomenon, hopefully what has been said in this book so far is enough to give you a framework for paying more attention to the relationships in your life.

Now, this isn't about struggling silently or suffering alone. This is about healing in a way that you feel great functioning on the foundation of your own two feet. This must be a priority because this is what will shift you from a consumer of energy to a provider of it. What this could look like is being able to share your gifts, talents, skills, and passions with the people around from a genuine place of love and generosity. This could manifest as a hobby, a project, volunteering, raising a family, being a leader in the workforce, or starting your own venture. Again, the options are absolutely endless, but I want to make it clear that this isn't a book for entrepreneurs about entrepreneurship. It is an example of how to go from low vibe to high vibe and raise the Collective vibe of humanity.

To evolve from being held captive in my marriage and being trafficked to captivating the hearts of others from stages all over the world required me to accept myself, my worth, and my purpose. It took courage to speak up, even though I knew it was possible that I might get it wrong. I often did. I stumbled over my words. I mispronounced for the whole world to see and yet, I'm here, I didn't die doing it. Captive and captivating are not adjectives to me. They are identities. They are potential ways of seeing yourself that will contribute to the story that you write about yourself.

Andrei has rewritten part of his story by coming out about his sexuality. The binary story that I had about him would have limited him and our relationship if I had insisted on holding onto it. Instead, I became willing to give up that story in order to make space for an empowering narrative with a lot more potential, options, and possibilities for a glorious future. We all have the potential to rewrite our story. I have been making a living out of that for the last few years and there is no end in sight to the work I get to do in the world.

When I first got to New Zealand, I decided that I was done being an employee. I wanted to work for myself and have the freedom to travel the world. I knew that I wanted to become a coach to really help people the way so many had helped me. Coaching was very appealing to me. I knew I could do this work from anywhere in the world and it was something I knew I would be good at, but I still had a few fears and insecurities in my way.

When I began my coach training program with HCI, Health Coaches Institute, I admired the other coaches on the stage and in my field lead and succeed. I noticed how articulate and fully alive they were and how they were making thousands of dollars in their businesses. I knew that I wanted to be a successful coach. I still have the picture my friend, Cassandra, took of me on stage pretending that I was the speaker. You better believe that I took that picture to put on my vision board.

I dreamt of speaking on stage but the voice in my head was too loud at first. "Who do you think you are? With your English?? You are still practicing words in the mirror for God's sake..." This only inspired me to do what I already knew to do: work hard. So, for the next year, I studied and worked even harder to qualify for the next level mastery program. I just knew that this was the next step for me. It was clear to me that this was my opportunity to create new evidence that I can and I'm capable, so I did.

When I began my coaching career, my focus was on parents, namely single parents. I was just getting started and my favorite way to describe the work I was doing was 'how to not fuck up your kids' coaching. It was really sophisticated. I was helping single parents be or become the parent their child needed. This work was important to me because of my own experience. Due to everything that I went through as a single parent, I learned how to not let my poor choices and my circumstances destroy my relationship with my son. Realizing that I was getting this parenting thing right was grounds for me to help other struggling families. I don't use the word 'right' a lot. It's way too absolute for me, but if I've only done one thing 'right' in my life, it's parenting, and I know how to not make others feel 'wrong' about their approach. Rather, I am willing to support, teach, and show a more constructive way.

The mastery program changed my life. Learning the coaching methods for myself helped me with my biggest limitation: my belief that I could never be successful with English as my second language. No matter how good of a coach I thought I might be, my English seemed to limit what I could say and do and this intimidated me from stepping fully into the identity. The work in the program and some amazing coaching helped me gain the confidence I needed to begin interviewing people around the world. I interviewed other entrepreneurs and leaders to learn from and later, I started my own podcast. On the show, I interviewed people from the LGBTQ community about their stories. By showing up consistently, I allowed myself to speak up without self-judgment, and never apologize for my English again.

This was a great start. My work developed into parenting classes, webinars, workshops, courses, and my first book. By following the natural flow of what was showing up for me, I ended up with a very family-oriented brand and business. This continued to evolve with my participation in the program and the work I was doing began to shift naturally as well. When I started to establish myself as a successful coach, other coaches came to me to ask how I was doing what I was doing.

My business was growing and I continued to do the work, participating in coaching events and attending business coaching retreats to make sure I'd keep learning. Connecting with other coaches and learning from my mentors at those events was a game changer for me. Making all this happen helped me realize my ability. I proved that small Self wrong as I found ways, with Dean's continued support, to travel from New Zealand to the United States for every live event. It was not easy, a short commute, or cheap, but it was so damn worth it because not only did I get more clear on my next step in business, but I discovered my revolution: to build a future where people from the LGBTQ community no longer need to come out of the closet. I decided to do my part in breaking all the labels and stereotypes and create an inclusive and loving future.

Because my focus had been on families, I hadn't exactly built anything around coaching other coaches and leaders in the LGBTQ community, but the process happened organically. What I knew was that my background in sales working with ING back in Romania taught me so many of the things I needed to know to be a successful coach and successfully present my work and my services. After seven years in America of feeling like I was always starting from scratch, I was able to directly apply my pre-existing knowledge to my American - and even my New Zealand - lifestyle. I took on other coaches and helped them succeed as well. It was so gratifying to come full circle and know that the work I had been doing for most of my life was worthwhile. This was a phase of my life and business that I really started to experience my vibe rising and my life elevating.

I'll be forever grateful for the training I received twenty plus years ago from ING collaboration. Our lessons are not always obvious when we are looping through that spiral. So often, we learn from the circumstances as we apply their lessons years and decades later. Always keep in mind that no lap around the loop is ever a waste. Always remember, every step matters!

As my career was growing rapidly, I knew that I had to put myself in front of cameras, do live videos, and get comfortable in interviews. I was running one hundred percent of my business online but I still did not feel ready to be seen on camera. I was not ready to be out of hiding just yet. This fear was absolutely paralyzing. I remember thinking and even saying, "forget about public speaking. There is no way in hell that I can do that," and yet I write to you now with a career as a global speaker, author, and leader. My one-on-one work with other coaches led me to opportunities for inclusivity consulting on a bigger scale. I kept working with other leaders in a way that kept opening doors for me. From these coaching and consulting relationships, my speaking career emerged.

I'd like to share with you the magic of the $10k in 10 weeks challenge organized by HCI. It was exactly as it sounded. We had to generate *ten thousand dollars* in ten weeks from coaching. The four finalists would get to speak live in front of the HCI tribe and the audience would vote on the winner.

And you guessed it, the winner gets a big, ten thousand dollar check. I still have mine up on my wall in the Spark Penthouse. In my first 10k challenge, I made exactly fifty dollars, but I reached my goal of writing and publishing my first book. This time, I wanted to make the full amount and overcome the fear of live videos. Therefore, I created my first group where I showed up for thirty consecutive days in live videos to support my clients, and it transformed my life in ways I could have never expected. The coaches in the program encouraged consistency and bold action and that scared the shit out of me. In my life, I knew the power of just talking action beyond your perceived limitations and I was willing to apply that lesson to my business. I was willing to stretch myself out of my comfort zone in business as well.

One day during this process, I woke up with an invitation to do a TEDx Talk. I said yes, before my fear kicked in, and believe me when I say, it definitely kicked in, big time! To this day, when I tell people that my first talk was on TEDx stage they don't believe it. Why? Because they can't comprehend exponential success. We have mostly been taught linear success that looks like, "we have to do this, then that, and maybe after x numbers of talks, if you're lucky enough, then you *might* get your big opportunity." I'm here as living proof that there are no rules!

Four days after my TEDx talk, as a finalist of the $10k Challenge having made over twenty thousand dollars in ten weeks, I delivered my second talk. I won the $10K Challenge for the Health Coaches Institute and won that big, sexy check for ten thousand dollars. I felt the momentum of my commitment pulling me through life towards massive success and recognition. During my time in the shelter, I wrote "I want to be famous." *This* was the kind of famous I had been dreaming about! My very specific definition of famous had manifested just as I had imagined it; standing on a big stage as a winner, with a big check in my hands. I am living *the dream* day in and day out.

As I became more well-known and established in my work, my path toward success unfolded right in front of me. I continued to get more involved in LGBTQ communities and received many invitations to speak on international stages. One of my most notable talks was given at The Surrogacy Conference in NZ, among fertility experts, my spouse included, from Australia, NZ, US, Europe, and Canada. Speaking and working with organizations developed into the world-changing work I will share in the upcoming chapters.

When I started this coaching journey, there were parts of me that would question 'do I belong? Who am I to do this? Am I good enough?" I would struggle with 'imposter syndrome' over and over at each level, but then, the more I succeeded, the more I gave that small Self dialogue up. I think that stretching past our insecurities is a natural and healthy phase of growing as a coach, and yet, it can be something that limits us if we always believe it. We must move past our limiting beliefs or upgrade them if we plan on being successful business people and making a powerful impact in the world. That also goes for being a successful parent, colleague, and friend.

I keep talking about success and being successful because I want to make it clear this is not about the money in the bank. Success is ultimately a state of mind, and for someone who wants to bring more movement to their life, success is whatever you define it as. It could be as simple as doing two push-ups or making two hundred dollars. It could be starting your book or podcast. It could be having that important conversation with your child or hitting your goal weight. You get to say what your success is and every step matters.

The same goes for leadership. Leaders come in all shapes and sizes with all sorts of paths and purposes. Going beyond our comfort zone is what allows us to experience our positive impact in the world. Outside of the comfort zone is where we find possibilities, opportunities, expansion, and magic.

The more I have stretched myself past my perceived limitations, the more positive impact I have been able to make in the world. I was becoming a change maker whose voice was getting louder and also being heard and listened to. All of this is available for each and every one of you when you say yes to yourself. Nine years ago, after calling a women's shelter home for five months, I dared to dream that one day I would have the freedom to create an impact in the world. I dared to write the details of my possible future on flashcards. Today, I am writing to you as a living testimony to possibility, as a coach who travels the world, who's now a TedX speaker, published author, founder of an online school, podcast host, and I did all of it in English, my second language.

Let that small voice in your head stay small. It cannot dream as big as you can. It is scared to go as far as you plan to. It cannot imagine how great things can be but that doesn't mean it has to stop you. Because I wasn't willing to stop when that small voice spoke up, I was able to make a global impact and will continue to for the rest of my days. When that voice in my head asks me "who do you think you are?" I answer, "I'm Simona Spark and I'm here to make a difference."

Chapter 19

Redefined

When I decided to raise my voice as a leader, I chose to speak up about sexual orientation and gender identification to a mainstream audience. I started by educating myself to be the parent that Andrei needed, not the parent I thought I was or wanted to be. For most parents, the top priority is about our child's welfare. Feed the baby, change the baby, clothe the baby. Keep the baby alive. So often, the question about "*who* is that baby?" doesn't ever come up. We, as parents, can get so wrapped up in our job of making sure our child has their physical needs met that we completely overlook their mental and emotional needs.

You may think that this advice is not for you if you are not a parent. Consider that as adults, we all have an impact in one way or another on the children in our lives. I'm talking to you, the adult. We all know that our children learn the most valuable traits like compassion, empathy, and love from us; their parents, their guardians. The children in our lives look up to us, the adults, and they learn from how we behave, regardless if you are a parent, a teacher, a neighbor, or just a friend of other parents. Children watch and learn much more than they listen and learn, especially when our words don't match our actions. We introduce the world to them through how we act, react and choose.

I saw all the ways that I, myself, was operating from the binary world of the male to female spectrum; except there wasn't much in between. When it came to sexuality, well, let's just say homosexuality wasn't even on my radar. You know enough about my Romanian history to probably guess that we didn't have much space available for any portion of the population that didn't fit the social norms. Therefore, my exposure and consideration was very low for how prevalent this concept was in the world or even right in my own home. My education in this matter was limited to, "gay men have sex with other men which puts them risk for incurable AIDS. Oh, and stay away from them because they are contagious."

My awareness about gender came later, as a mom, when I was met with binary stereotypes around clothing, colors, and toys. I didn't feel right, yet I didn't have enough knowledge to take a stand for it. I remember receiving a gift for my son, a gun toy, and I refused it. I was both taking a stand against guns and violence. Even though the other person was saying, "boys like to play with guns, it's a toy for boys," I had no interest in him having a toy gun.

Moving to the US gave me access to a more open-minded culture, and I made friends with amazing people from the LGBTQ community. These new connections opened my eyes and mind and allowed me to support my child by raising him from a place of inclusivity and acceptance of all humans—no matter race, gender, sexual orientation, nationality, etc. All people are capable of love and deserve to be loved.

I was not upset or disturbed by Andrei's coming out and opening up to me about his sexual orientation. I had a feeling about it and a few times, I tried to 'set the stage' for him to come out, and yet, you never know one hundred percent until your child is claiming it. With all that inclusive mindset I still had some learning to do if I wanted to make space for a healthy conversation on this topic. It meant that I had to consider beliefs and truths other than what I had been shown and this is the case for so many parents and individuals as they begin to blur the lines between male and female or gay and straight.

I started having daily and weekly appointments with the all-knowing 'Dr. Google,' and he had so much information for me. I contacted some of my gay friends and asked questions that I had never asked before. As I began my own research, I made discoveries that inspired me to begin teaching and speaking on the topic. It also ignited my passion for normalizing this conversation in this world, which is exactly what I aim for with my *Redefined Family in the Modern Age of LGBTQ* Podcast. All that work brought me to the opportunity to give a TEDx Talk about my idea, which apparently was worth spreading: 'A Gender for Every Human Body." I invited my audience to consider that there could be as many gender identities and sexual orientations as there are people in the world: over seven and half billion.

I invite you to imagine this world without gender labels of 'man' and 'woman.' I won't do a whole class on gender identity here, but know that when I say gender, I'm referring to the whole gender identity. Before we move forward, I'll explain the difference between sex and gender, in the most simplified way I know how: the way that I explain it in my workshops with teens. Sex is between your legs, and gender is between your ears.

That being said, the gender identity has all these components: sex assigned at birth, sexual expression, sexual orientation, and sexual attraction. Beyond that, consider that there may be a gender identity for every individual human body. We have been pretty comfortable letting everyone know about how unique and special they are *and still* expect them to only identify with one of two groups: men or women. This seems like a conflicting message; you can be anything you want as long as you are part of one of the two: man or woman.

We all have a unique mix of masculine and feminine energy. We have varying strengths, weaknesses, preferences, and desires, and they are not gender specific. They are human specific. This is what creates our unique individuality and personality. We will be able to meet people for who they actually are when we accept that who and how we are isn't solely dependent upon the sex or gender we identify with.

If we pay more attention to who a person is, we can see each other for the energy that creates our personalities and talents instead of being labeled as not feminine or masculine enough. We know men who like to paint, cook, sing, and raise children. We know women who thrive in the workforce, on the field, and at the front of the line. This is all acceptable. We broke the idea stereotype of gender specific jobs, sports, and hobbies a long time ago. This diversity is important to the fabric of our society. There is a yin and yang balance caused by the ways in which we are different and I enjoy speaking on the importance of allowing and celebrating the differences between us.

When our strengths and skills no longer have to be categorized as gender specific, there is an opportunity for each person to explore their authentic nature. People are given the freedom to expand their feminine and masculine energy as much as it feels right for them to become who they are meant to be. There is no tool to measure masculine or feminine energy or to determine what is too much of this or not enough of that. It is not necessary, so I began to wonder what all the fuss was about with the need to identify it. In all my research, I have asked, "why do we need to identify and categorize?"

When I began to explore this idea, I began to wonder who decided what clothing, toys, hobbies, and jobs were for each gender. Who said "these are men's preferences" and "these are women's preferences?" Who decided which colors were for boys and girls? Seriously, who? I want to meet that person! Okay, okay, I know the truth is that this is a culmination of generations' worth of conditioning, but I know that part of my purpose of the planet is to break up these limiting stories and stereotypes that keep people in the limitations of gender roles. If we remove the labels, we won't see genders in pinks and blues, but rather, in rainbows.

In fact, the perfect example of how many genders there can be is comparable to the rainbow pride flag. The pride flag was designed in 1978 by the artist Gilbert Baker, an openly gay man and a drag queen. The colors he chose were specific and have meaning; hot pink for sex, red for life, orange for healing, yellow for sunlight, green for nature, turquoise for art, indigo for harmony, and violet for spirit. The mathematician and most influential scientist of all time, Isaac Newton, was the first to identify the colors of the rainbow. The specific number of colors we learn are ROYGBIV; red, orange, yellow, green, blue, indigo, and violet. We learn this on the most basic level on paper, but when you get a glimpse of a rainbow in real life, there are so many tones of each that we can no longer identify the exact colors, just its beauty. You could look at the variety of genders similar to looking at the rainbow.

I believe that the most important thing about living in a world without gender labels, is that families will become a safe space for children to explore their courageous personalities, get curious about their bodies, and learn about love. As a result, children have a better opportunity to grow up with a strong sense of inclusivity among their families and peers.

If you meet me in person, read my books, watch my talks and videos, or tune into any of my content, you might gather that my main message is unconditional love. I might say it a million different ways with about fifteen dozen stories, but the message is always love. If I stretch you, it's from love. If I question you, it's from love. If I call you out on your BS, it's from love. If I put a flashlight on parts you're hiding, it's from love. No matter what, love is always the answer and it is always the energy to operate from. I have made this my life's mission and so in these last few chapters, I will share a bit more about how I have taken on redefining labels and love in this world.

I plainly explain my mission of love so you can knowingly jump on board and take the ride with me. I am not about being subtle or discrete. I am not interested in surprising you, but rather, consciously bringing you along for the journey. One of my major goals is to put the power back in your hands. I have spent a whole book sharing my story so that you might take a closer look at yours. I like to tell my clients, "copy/paste, and make it your own." So please, take what resonates with you, apply it in your life, and support others to do the same.

Look in your life at where you are not practicing unconditional love and consider what is in the way of that. What is blocking you from giving and receiving love, fully? Focus especially on the receiving part; this can be a tricky one! Living in love is an inside job. It requires willingness to release the shame, guilt, and fear. It takes courage to express our desires as well as face our anger and pride. We must learn to forgive and accept ourselves and others.

When it comes to redefining love, consider the way you have already defined it. What constitutes someone worthy of your love? Who doesn't qualify? Imagine a world where we all took one hundred percent responsibility for the way we love and became more willing to give it out more freely.

My son coming out was a gift for me. It opened my eyes and made me realize the limiting beliefs, barriers, and blind spots of my love. It took me to a deeper level than I have ever been before. This gave me a real, tangible opportunity to expand myself to be as loving as I thought I already was. This stretched me to love fully which has set me free in so many ways. Over the years of taking on this work, my heart has begun to feel lighter and I have started to feel more alive. My life has become richer in this process and I am so passionate about sharing this wisdom and perspective to give everyone an opportunity to live this freely and fully.

Taking on this work on a personal scale can still make a global difference. Maybe you don't have dreams and goals like mine to speak all over the world or publish multiple books to make an impact. Loving the people right in front of you is just as important, powerful, and impactful. Each one of us could support a world without labels and it starts inside of our homes. If we stay committed to this, our ripple effect will be endless and effortless. As parents, we raise our future. We have the power to create a future filled with love and acceptance. We are the ones setting the example. My child could become friends with your child. I think it is safe to assume that you and I both want our children to be treated with love, respect, inclusivity and acceptance. *We* get to teach them that!

I am going to spend the rest of this chapter boiling down the work there is to do in the area of unconditional love so that you can take this work on for yourself. As I shared previously about my process of forgiveness, I had to learn to love myself above all things or people. Raising my vibe was impossible while also hating myself. Those two things don't go together.

When I tried to fit into my own experience of a binary world, this looked like: good mom vs bad mom; obedient daughter vs disgraceful daughter; submissive wife vs embarrassing wife; conformist or rebel. I functioned on opposite ends of a spectrum that had very little in-between and this kept me locked into disempowering habits and patterns.

For a while, I looked at all judgments as negative, but then I started to question that. I wondered to myself, "Why does judgment always have to be considered negative? Couldn't there be positive judgments, too?" So I shifted my mindset away from *right vs wrong* judgment. This helped me release the judgment and allowed me the contrast to *just be*, because what's right for me might be considered wrong for you. This created a lot of freedom and I invite you to give it a try as well. Release any idea of the way things should be and accept them for how they are.

The way my binary beliefs were set up limited my range of emotional motion and stunted my growth. This probably explains why I am so short. I have been limited in so many ways for most of my life that raising my voice over the last few years has made me feel taller — bigger than ever. I felt deserving of taking space in the world. Maybe even larger than life.

Not in that egotistical way but in the limitless, inexhaustible kind of way. When someone tells me something can't be done, I tell them I already fired the word 'challenge' and move on. When I hear stories about division, blame, shame, and hatred, I look for where the love is missing or hidden. This helps me discover a resolution quickly and efficiently. I am a leader for this reason, and you can be too.

I cannot speak about unconditional love if I am not practicing it. Unity cannot be my message if I am not creating it in and around me. We cannot live in harmony if we are unwilling to unconditionally accept each other for who we naturally are. This work starts with us.

When I started to bend the rules of identification, I let myself consider that I wasn't a bad mom, disgraceful daughter, embarrassing wife, or selfish rebel. I had to see another side of people's judgments. This was a game changer for me. I outgrew that identity of who I used to be. I outgrew the belief system I had been raised in. During that trip to Romania in 2015, when I realized the voices in my head weren't mine, I was able to consider who I might be by my own definition.

I felt so much struggle with these judgments because deep down, I *knew* they weren't true or accurate. Instead of understanding their falseness, I struggled with whatever the feeling the judgments caused. Because I was locked in the emotions of shame, doubt, and worthlessness, I could not handle this situation. I had to exit my own binary brain to see anything new become available. The concept 'polarity' took on a new meaning to me. I had been using a right and wrong, good and bad, black and white type of mindset, and decided to embrace more of the contrast between positive and negative. Instead of judging anything, I just began to observe. This opened my mind and world.

When I first read those self-help books, ten years ago, that reframed speaking up and standing your ground as powerful, my brain started to change. When those books redefined leaving as knowing when enough is enough, I felt seen and understood. I saw that maybe I wasn't selfish or disgraceful but I could possibly be courageous and smart. This opened up my world the same way Andrei did when he came out.

Only looking back can I see that I recognized what he was doing. He was redefining himself the same way I had. People and society had decided a lot about me that wasn't true for me. I had decided a lot about him that wasn't true for him. Had I not recreated my own identity before, I may have not had the capacity for his shift.

Think of something you are already good at. Generally, you could teach someone else about it or how to do it. It is each of our own duty to get good at accepting ourselves. When we accept ourselves, for our strengths, weaknesses, attributes, and downfalls, we can certainly accept others as they navigate themselves and life. This makes us leaders of love who can teach and guide others along the way.

Something that I have gotten really good at is no longer hiding or running. I have learned that when triggered about something or someone, that trigger is nothing but an invitation to look inward and see what parts of yourself need to be heard, seen, forgiven, healed, and loved. I love my triggers and got really good at putting myself in uncomfortable spaces where triggers might show up, because I'm no longer going to hide myself; I'm willing to face all the parts of me.

This is exactly what I mean by this work starting with you. We can only meet others as deeply as we have met ourselves. We must take on this work in order to make any lasting difference in our homes, communities, or the world. If we do, we can create a unified world even in the face of our differences and actually embrace everyone as unique gifts that enrich our lives. Differences are like unique spices that bring unique flavor that make our world tastier. We can contribute to a world that celebrates the differences of humanity and encourages authentic expression.

If we let every person raise their authentic voice, there will be a harmony that will sound like an orchestra, each instrument playing their unique part, coming together to become a symphony, raising humanity to the frequency of love. I believe this is possible, and I have dedicated my life to moving us in that direction. We can reframe 'differences' into 'gifts.' We can redefine love, acceptance, and celebration. We can create peace.

Chapter 20
Redefined Family

One of my strangest out-of-body experiences was standing alone in a round room with walls covered in floor-to-ceiling mirrors in a bathroom at a five hundred-plus person conference in Taipei, Taiwan in 2018. It was strange, because I could have stood there all day and only encountered one or two other females. I have been to a lot of events in my day and have never been to one where there wasn't a line to the ladies' bathroom. This is a unique experience, worth mentioning, worth celebrating; don't you agree?

The Men Having Babies Non-Profit Organization was founded in New York in 2005 to help gay men who desired to be parents create their family through surrogacy. At the time of their establishment in the late nineties, gay men were not allowed to become parents. Much the opposite, they were harshly ridiculed, discriminated against, and denied equal rights.

The most beautiful thing to witness was five hundred men determined and willing to go through any and every obstacle to become parents. It was astonishing to be in a room with this group talking about this topic. Never in my life have I been in an environment surrounded by so much love, selflessness, and commitment. I could feel it with every fiber of my being and it sent ice up my spine to be in their presence. I was honored to be invited and granted access to this powerful experience and am forever grateful to the Founder, Ron Poole-Dayan, for having me there.

It was at this conference that I learned the distinction of coming out vs coming home. In Western culture, claiming your identity is a person's right. This is about the individual and *may* result in rejection and separation. In Asian culture, coming out is a very intimate process about protecting the family structure and continuing to exist in that family unit. So, it is not about '*me.*' It is more about *us.* "Coming home" is bringing the partner *into* the family and being accepted by the family. This, of course, can occur in Western culture as well, but the situation is often more dire in Eastern culture, as being gay is still not widely accepted. Protection of family means everything and coming home was exactly how I felt for Andrei when he opened up to me.

Another interesting difference that I noticed was that in Western culture we are most accustomed to seeing single moms. In contrast, there are a lot of men who intend to be single fathers in Asian culture. While at this conference, these men shared about how raising their voices, speaking their truths, and unleashing their hearts led them to a place of peace and acceptance that most of them had never felt hiding in the closet, my own heart felt unleashed. Gay or not, I related to the liberation of speaking up and standing out. This is just one example but this conference completely demolished out-dated paradigms and began creating new ones for me. A whole world of possibility, a new level of acceptance, and the deepest level of unconditional love in creating a family was opening up right before my very eyes.

At the time of the conference in Taipei, same-sex marriage and, of course, gay couple parenting, were not supported by their government. The men who attended came together and supported each other in the movement toward equality. This MHB organization has transformed the world of same-sex parenting litigation in so many senses. When I interviewed Ron as a guest on my podcast, I learned how life was for him and his partner twenty years ago when they wanted to create their family. I later interviewed his daughter and she shared how her dads addressed the school forms to read Parent 1 and Parent 2 as opposed to Mother and Father. They have played a role in the rights of gay parents all over the world. They have continued for decades in supporting gay men who intend to be parents around the world. I don't know exactly what role they played in Taiwan but I do know that about one year after this conference, same-sex marriage legality was passed in Taiwan.

The love, passion, commitment, peace, collaboration, trust, and faith of these men was enough to move mountains that had been set in place since the dawn of their civilizations. To say that I was inspired by these men would be a complete understatement. These men are building a better future for my son and I have no words to express my gratitude. Their courage gave me clarity about what I was raising my voice about at my own conferences and talks.

Redefining the definition of a 'proper' family structure being a mom, a dad, and two children was what I had set out to do. My passion to normalize a conversation about the variety of the family unit was reinforced by participating in this Men Having Babies conference. It helped me get even more clear on my work and added fuel to my fire to keep raising my voice about this transition.

Seeing five hundred men show up fully for fatherhood made me want to fight for each and every one of their rights to love children and give them amazing homes. LGBTQ intending parents and families experience so many more challenges than the traditional family when it comes to creating their own family. The journey to create a baby is definitely not a straight line to the goal.

I can probably go on a tangent about how many straight parents provide broken or dysfunctional homes but are never questioned, simply because of their heterosexuality. Same-sex couples don't become parents by accident. LGBTQ families must go through the complicated processes of IVF and surrogacy. That includes extra tests, collecting, freezing, and donating eggs and sperm, choosing a surrogate, adoption procedures, lawyers, and so much more. It's a bit more complicated than just having great sex and nine months later, here's your baby! I love to say that kids of LGBTQ parents can know *for sure* that they were wanted. There is no mistake about that. We have loving people in the world being denied the right to love and this breaks my heart. As we know, creating a family is just one of many areas of life the LGBTQ community faces resistance in.

According to the Anxiety and Depression Association of America, up to sixty percent of LGBTQ individuals suffer from anxiety and depression because of their gender identity and sexual orientation. Forty percent of gay or transgender adults are reported to have made a suicide attempt, with ninety-two percent of these individuals doing so before the age of twenty-five, as reported in the Trevor project.

There are examples of this growing issue in every country and culture. There are examples that make headlines, like kids who are bullied so badly for being gay that they take their own life. There are thousands of cases that never make the news or even a day-to-day conversation. Like a wildfire, this problem grows because the majority of the population is not willing or able to tame it. We are not acknowledging the roots of bullying and suicide being the unspoken expectations and limitations that a binary world puts on people. A few days before my TEDx Talk, "A Gender for Every Human Body," the local newspaper had a headline on the front page about parents revolting against schools because they "teach their children to be gay." I was worried. No, I was scared. All I could think was, "This is Colorado. People have guns and I'm about to go live on stage in front of these locals with a message for parents to parent from a place of inclusion." I was afraid to my core.

Children are a direct product of their environment, and the environments we are providing our children are not one's that cultivate love, acceptance, and unconditional love. We often teach our little ones judgment, prejudice, and division. Too often, children don't even need to leave their home to learn how to reject others. They witness it among family members or are the one being rejected, neglected, or bullied. Acceptance and inclusivity is the adult's responsibility and I am also very aware that many adults grew up in the same home environments that they are now creating, or much worse.

I can completely relate to this and I believe this is so much of where my passion comes from. I do not believe parents have the right to raise children in dysfunctional homes just because they, themselves were. I also believe that we have a responsibility to end the cycle of pain, trauma, and karmic debt. My loving word of advice to all parents, and adults for that matter, who are struggling with their own childhood trauma, is to heal. Our children do not inherently deserve to suffer the ways we did. This does not mean that we need to make life entirely easy for them. Let's not confuse abuse with discipline and love with lack of boundaries. It means we offer them a clean slate and a strong foundation from which to build their own life from; a foundation of unconditional love, kindness, generosity, and fellowship.

I can relate to growing up in a dysfunctional family and having dysfunctional marriages. Doing what we can to end the pattern is our work. The work I have mentioned starts here, with us. Healing, feeling, forgiving, and releasing are necessities to living a full life and raising a functional family, no matter what the structure of that family is. If love is present, anyone can thrive. By opening up the spectrum of gender labels and sexual orientation, we can help our children feel safe, loved, and welcomed. We can create a future where everyone is loved for who they are. This is where shifting the focus to biology and love, over gender roles and laws, can be incredibly beneficial for our families.

When we change the conversation from laws to love, we can see that there really are no laws *to* love. Love is love and it surpasses all boundaries and definitions. When we move the focus to biology over gender labels or sexual orientation, the most important thing to teach our children is that they are born with a body filled with incredible parts.

Teaching biology over stereotypes will lay the foundation to teach them how their own bodies function instead of how society functions. When we consider that everyone is able to have their own gender identities and preferences, we can begin to accept everyone's right to love any person they choose. We can honor each individual's freedom whomever they wish and their right to create their own family together.

We get to create a family with anyone we choose, regardless of their sex. Science supports this idea by proving that in order to create another human, all that is required is one sperm, one egg, a place for them to mix together, and *poof*, you got yourself a baby. It's not magic, it's science, and it is available to us no matter who our partner is and no matter what our family looks like.

In my work of sharing this message with the world, I began my own personal research by interviewing individuals from LGBTQ community across the globe. I would have them on my podcast to share their story and this gave me a chance to ask the questions that I had. This also created an opportunity for other people who were curious to educate themselves on this topic. Furthermore, these interviews served as the bridge for many people struggling to communicate with friends and family that did not understand their sexual orientation or gender identification. My podcast has been one of my favorite personal and professional projects that I am so grateful to have produced. It grew me in many ways and has contributed to a powerful conversation in the world. I saw this message spreading and more people opening up to new ways of living that can and has liberated millions.

In my research, I learned about children who were put in the streets by their own parents for being gay. I heard about people who stayed in heterosexual marriages for decades, until they found the strength to come out. I know of countless transgender individuals who have lost everything and everyone when claiming their truth, but also stories of people who were held, loved, and supported on their journey. These are the true and unspoken stories of so many. In each case, the conversation is about people's capacity and willingness to accept and love unconditionally. These stories took my breath away and added even more fuel to my fire of sharing the message of unconditional love.

All children deserve the chance to grow up to be who they are meant to become. As we grow and evolve, we all change and transform, but love is available no matter what. No one needs to look or act a certain way to deserve love and affinity. As parents, we don't get to love our children unconditionally *only* if they meet our expectations. This includes all the "pro-life" religious groups, who claim to love life so much, but the love stops if the child comes out as gay. Parents, if you say you love your children, then love your children, even when they might exist or act differently than you think is "normal." They especially don't have to be denied love just because they don't fit a certain mold or meet our standards.

So parents, let's love our children fully, truly, and unconditionally, by allowing them to grow into who they are meant to become. Let's teach them about love as if love doesn't know color, gender, or social status. I will ask you to consider, what if there could be over seven and a half billion gender identities in the world. What if everyone were truly free to love who and how they want?

We could strip away all the labels and focus on the expression of love through the power of inclusivity. We could redefine the family structure. We could redefine the norms and expectations on a societal level. Doing so could lead to not just functional homes, but a functional world where peace, love, acceptance, and harmony are available.

This is a world I would like to live in and watch my son enjoy. This is a world I believe in and dedicate my life to creating. This is a world that includes all living and loving beings and makes room for everyone. Imagine that world.

Chapter 21

Raising YOUR Voice

We have made it to the last few pages, my friend. I know I said it on page one, but would you consider us friends now? We have been through a lot together and for you to have made it to this page of the book, I would consider you someone that I feel aligned with and connected to. I want to thank you and acknowledge you for arriving here.

Raising My Voice: The Memoir of an Immigrant has been a project of the heart and soul, in the works for forty-four years, and I am sure it is no mistake that it has made its way into your life. I imagine that you are committed to a world that promotes inclusion, acceptance, and unconditional love. Prioritizing these concepts is what makes you, you and what makes me, me. Naturally, that makes us *we*.

We are on a clear mission to create healthier relationships, empower individuals, and raise the frequency of humanity. This is no small task and it will take a unified front to do so. We are way stronger together than we are alone. We must come together in our process of healing, and include each other in that journey. Raising my voice and writing this book was intended to cause an important conversation about what inclusion can look and feel like.

Through sharing my own life and experience, I spent this book divulging my stories, perspectives, hopes, dreams, and visions, and I will always invite you to do the same. I invite you to raise your voice high. This can look any way that inspires you.

You can start in your relationships, in your home, at work, at church, and more. You can start online or in person or over the phone. My invitation to you is to come out of whatever closet you hide out in and live your truth. This can be about sexual orientation and gender identification, or not. You might finally realize and admit that you don't want to live up to other people's expectations of you. You might follow your desire for a drastic career switch that allows you to express your passion more. The possibilities are endless.

My main invitation to you is to raise your voice and live out loud. I invite you to love yourself fully and allow yourself to be loved. I understand this can be a tall task for those of us who have been hurt and harmed by others, and I am here to encourage you anyway. Prove yourself wrong about the way people are and venture out to find your tribe.

When I risked it all and took my chance to come to the United States of America, every day, I became closer and closer to living a full life. It was by thrusting myself out of what was familiar that I was able to discover all that was available. I am so grateful that I did and I want to always shine light on the possibility of you finding that level of happiness and fulfillment, too. We all deserve it and it is within arms' reach if we are willing to reach out.

My intention with this book for you is that you accept all these invitations for yourself so that you are fully unleashed to be a thriving example of love in the world. May your passion be reignited to step out and step up for your role in the evolution of humanity. We all need each other out there and there is no way we can arrive home without every last one of us walking in the same direction.

In this marathon of life there is no one winner. The race is over when each and every one of us crosses the finish line so our responsibility is to not leave anyone behind but honor everyone's speed and pace. This means dropping judgments, forgiving, and finding love, even in the people who have hurt and harmed us. This is where the freedom we all seek lies. Complete detachment from the wrongdoings of others opens up the door to the next phase of our life.

That next phase is one of purpose and passion. Being healed creates space for what you really care about and energizes you in a way that you can show up for it fully and on fire. I look forward to hearing from you to find out how raising your voice improved the quality and direction of your life.

My dear friend, you deserve everything good and more. You deserve love and prosperity and you will be the one to give it to yourself and this world by opening up that beautiful heart of yours. Thank you for opening your heart and mind to me and my story. Thank you for opening up your schedule to read about the life and times of an immigrant looking to find a place she belongs.

I have found the place where I always wanted to plant my roots; in my own heart, and have grown a beautiful life straight from the center of my chest. I let myself grow, bloom, and blossom by tending to my needs and watering my dreams. The garden of life is a great one and success is always in season. With that, I would like to share one last poem with you.

Human Nature

Spring, summer, winter, fall
Are the seasons of your souls
Mother nature teach us once
This is the circle of our lives

Like the nature, your soul too
Has the seasons going through
Don't even try to control
It's a process, helps you grow

Take a minute, see the truth
All of this applies to you
Doesn't matter where you are
Into this circle you always are

When everything goes well and right
All around you looks so bright
You have summer in your soul
Always smiling, feel no cold

For some reason after that
Leaf's start shaking and in the end
Fall apart, leaving the trees
And you find yourself in tears

All the warmth become to cold
And feel empty like a hole
Have no idea, feel no hope
Winter's here. It's so cold

Then from nowhere, you just see
A ray of sun, and then some green
Spring time knock on your soul's door
Bringing the hope and so much more

Everything's so clear now
Nothing can't put you down
You know exactly what to do
It's summer time again for you

Try accept your destiny
Work your seasons carefully
You'll become a better person
It's no secret, it's human nature.

It is in our human nature to grow, love, and serve. It is our destiny to thrive. Everything becomes clear when we follow the guidance of our hearts and the authenticity of our own voice.

Thank you for joining me on this journey; it is an honor to serve you on yours.

I look forward to the next time when our paths cross. Until then, spark your transformation by raising your voice and share your unique gifts with the world.

Much love,

Simona

Paper Never Forgets!

What have you discovered about yourself
reading this book?

Resources

1. **Author: Simona Spark** www.simonaspark.com
   - email: transformation@simonaspark.com
   - **No More Messy Kids: The Spark Method- when cleaning is a choice and not a chore** - by Simona Spark - available on amazon https://tinyurl.com/s9322z2u
   - **Raising My Voice Community-** Facebook Group https://www.facebook.com/groups/raisingmyvoice/
   - **Redefined Family in the modern age of LGBTQ Podcast** Spotify https://open.spotify.com/show/2XgjByFgam3oiVSb3Ev-B3u?si=2vC4-aEhRbGcq4MyEMVB7w iTune https://podcasts.apple.com/us/podcast/redefined-family-in-the-modern-age-of-lgbtq/id1440327736
   - **Spark Transformation Academy** www.sparktransformation.academy
   - **TEDx Talk:** A Gender For Every Human Body - YouTube, TED https://www.ted.com/talks/simona_spark_a_gender_for_every_human_body https://www.youtube.com/watch?v=9Y3uEojdd2U

2. **Bauer Law Firm, LL** catherine@rochesterimmigration.com

3. **Bill Baren** - Business Oracle www.billbaren.com IG @billbaren

4. **Hearts Unleashed Podcast** https://www.heartsunleashed.com

5. **Health Coach Institute** www.healthcoachinstitute.com

6. **Inner Coach** www.innercoach.com

7. **It's Not Human Sexuality Podcast** https://lkbthwys.podbean.com

8. **Look Both Ways, Inc.** www.lkbthwys.org

9. **Men Having Babies** www.menhavingbabies.org

10. **Thought Leader Academy** www.saraconnell.com/TLANew

About the Author

From an immigrant with no identification to a global citizen and gender identity activist, Simona Spark has turned her passion for equality into her full-time career as a coach, author, and speaker. After finding herself homeless and living in a women's shelter, she has learned how to help others turn their greatest challenges into their greatest gifts.

As the CEO & Founder of *Spark Transformation Academy*, Simona works with people from all walks of life, supporting them to release limiting beliefs so they can fully embrace their identity and create the future they desire and deserve. She also works with coaches, mentors, and advocates to help them discover their purpose and build businesses that align with their heart's mission and message.

As the host of the *Redefined Family in the Modern Age of LGBTQ Podcast*, she is committed to creating a future free from labels and stereotypes. Simona has made a career of teaching people how to elevate their lives by raising their voices and she shares those stories with her worldwide audience.

As the author of *No More Messy Kids* (2018), she guides parents into becoming the role models their children need in building life skills in a natural and effortless manner. In *Raising My Voice: The Memoir of an Immigrant* (2021), through sharing her own experiences, Spark teaches readers how to speak up, speak out, and come out through healing, owning, and sharing their own story.

As an immigrant from a communist country, Simona faced gender barriers, discrimination, and even domestic violence. In a commitment to herself and her son for a greater life, she took a chance and came to the United States to pursue the American dream. During her journey from speaking no English to standing on the TEDx stage, she has relied on her commitment to her vision to raise herself above her circumstances to charge forth into her destiny.

Born and raised in Romania, Simona's journey has moved her to sixteen addresses, in six countries and states, on three different continents. She now resides in Los Angeles, California.